The Twilight Years

The Twilight Years

Biblical Hermeneutics of Ageism
with an Asian Perspective on Aging

GILBERT SOO HOO

WIPF & STOCK · Eugene, Oregon

THE TWILIGHT YEARS
Biblical Hermeneutics of Ageism with an Asian Perspective on Aging

Copyright © 2024 Gilbert Soo Hoo. All rights reserved. Except for brief quotations in critical publications or reviews, no part of this book may be reproduced in any manner without prior written permission from the publisher. Write: Permissions, Wipf and Stock Publishers, 199 W. 8th Ave., Suite 3, Eugene, OR 97401.

Wipf & Stock
An Imprint of Wipf and Stock Publishers
199 W. 8th Ave., Suite 3
Eugene, OR 97401

www.wipfandstock.com

PAPERBACK ISBN: 979-8-3852-0757-2
HARDCOVER ISBN: 979-8-3852-0758-9
EBOOK ISBN: 979-8-3852-0759-6

VERSION NUMBER 02/28/24

Quoting previously published materials in this work falls within "fair use." All quotes used are acknowledged and credited in the associated footnotes.

All Scripture quotations are taken from the New American Standard Bible. Copyright 1960, 1971, 1977, 1995, 2020 by The Lockman Foundation. Used by permission. All rights reserved. www.lockman.org

Contents

Preface | vii

Acknowledgments | ix

Abbreviations | x

Introduction | xi

CHAPTER 1
A Global Phenomenon and Challenge | 1

CHAPTER 2
Biblical Hermeneutics of Ageism | 23

CHAPTER 3
Summarizing the Principles of the Biblical Hermeneutics of Ageism | 58

CHAPTER 4
Specific Scriptural References to Old Age | 63

CHAPTER 5
Old Age according to the Wisdom Literature | 80

CHAPTER 6
Concluding Thoughts | 114

Bibliography | 129

Preface

FOR SEVERAL YEARS I perused the photos of and notes from former classmates in high school through the social platform Classmates.com. If ever we participate in a class reunion, it would commemorate nearly sixty years since graduation. The reality of the passage of time already hit hard when I checked out some books from the local library over twenty years before. The librarian recognized me by name, but I remained clueless as to her identity until she told me her maiden name. Then I took a careful look at her and a vague resemblance of her youth emerged. Now more time has passed and I don't look much like I did at the library.

The subject of old age is a deeply personal one, as I am constantly reminded by the mirror that I am far into that phase of life I used to think only applied to others. But as I continue to read government and other official reports, I find that I am part of an increasing global phenomenon. No geographical region is exempted. Not surprisingly many people have written about this topic. So what justifies me adding to the steadily growing literature? I offer at least two reasons. One, I propose a biblical hermeneutics of ageism for Christian readers seeking the Bible's view on old age. Through this hermeneutical framework, I hope to avoid unwarranted moralization of the text, making it proclaim whatever one wishes, and proof texting, taking verses out of context and, essentially, having the Bible support any position one fancies. Hence, a biblical hermeneutics enables Scripture to have its own voice. Second, since old age is global, I insert an Asian worldview on the topic. Cultural distinctives require a nuanced approach to accommodate a broader range of concerns, practices, and beliefs as we survey different regions. However, the multifaceted characteristics of the Asian region, each with its own culture, beliefs and values, life and family practices and dynamics, imply that the danger of generalizing the traits of one region to cover the traits of other regions is very real and to be avoided. I investigate six different Asian regions and present my findings about those regions without attempting to stereotype by stating "this is what Asians do" without qualification. Six regions represent only a fraction of Asia. Likewise, when I comment about Western views, I specifically mean views that arise in the USA and not those in Europe or Canada.

I visualize one major objective of my investigation is alerting churches to the fact their members are aging and that potentially changes the dynamics of doing church. Simply being aware that senior citizens compose an ever-larger percentage of the congregation is not enough. Vision-casting, planning, and ministry involving and directed to older members should be intentional. Do they feel that their concerns and challenges occupy the significant attention of their leaders? Do they feel that they are an important part of the church? And perhaps a more important question is: Are they indeed a vital and appreciated segment of the body of Christ?

As an important first step toward addressing these questions, the present volume offers a roadmap toward reading the Bible from the point of view of ageism. When Scripture is read accordingly, the church and its leaders can be more in the forefront of addressing this global phenomenon. This volume can also serve seminaries and Bible schools in Asia and the West in the training of future pastors, missionaries, and Christian leaders. More broadly, concerned Christians everywhere should aspire to become more Bible-literate, not only in the general sense but, in particular, to become more sensitive to their older brothers and sisters in the family of God.

Acknowledgments

THE DIFFICULT MONTHS FOLLOWING my "retirement" from theological education were a shocker. During that period, I experienced to the fullest extent the difference between cognition and affect. Intellectually, I knew the inevitable transition from full-time to part-time would arrive as I observed others near my age stepping down. I was even forewarned the previous year that my contract would not be renewed. But the accompanying emotional roller coaster, when it was my time, caused turmoil within. Fortuitously, my wife Ming recognized my symptoms, being a professional counselor, and guided and encouraged me as I pushed through. As a lifelong partner, she and I have journeyed from our young adult years, first dating and then marriage, through the middle years of raising a family, and now in our later years and beyond. The journey continues. We believe that fruitful years still lay ahead. We dream and plan together, trying to envision our next adventure. Life is far from over.

Thank you, Ming, for getting me back on my feet and traveling again. This book is a testament to your love, wisdom, and companionship. I also acknowledge our children, Weiki and Winyan, for delighting us with your own adventures and adding meaning to our lives. I recall one episode many years ago when my daughter was perhaps six or seven and spoke some endearing words to me. She said, "Daddy, you're not getting old." I was so touched for a split second. Then she added, "You're already old." Sigh. How can I forget?!

Abbreviations

AB	The Anchor Bible
ADB	Asian Development Bank
EBC	The Expositor's Bible Commentary
IVP	InterVarsity Press
JBL	Journal of Biblical Literature
NICNT	The New International Commentary on the New Testament
NICOT	The New International Commentary on the Old Testament
RACP	The Royal Australasian College of Physicians
SBL	Society of Biblical Literature
SWD	Social Welfare Department

Introduction

THE GLOBAL PHENOMENON OF an aging population characterizes virtually all major geographical regions of the world. Even though the aged may still represent a minority, they are a growing minority that cannot be ignored. The aging trend has captured the attention of governments, corporations, and even citizens on the street. Both the old and the young, largely because of their aged relatives, seem preoccupied. All of this leads to some questions that demand answers and influence a nuanced investigation.

The first question is obvious: What is considered old age? Surprisingly, people offer different responses, ranging from reaching the decade of 60 and older, or more specifically 65, often regarded as the age of retirement, but with workers delaying retirement, that age-delimiter varies as some continue working at 70 and beyond. Others offer more qualitative answers: "When I can no longer do things I used to do"; "It takes me longer to recover from some exertion like exercise"; "I don't have the energy I once had"; or "People regard me as old." I personally resonate with this last response—when gray-haired strangers publicly call me "uncle," a customary Asian greeting that displays courtesy and respect toward those seen as older rather than as something derogatory. Then how can I deny that I am now old, especially if my wife tells me directly, "You're an old man."

In recent decades, achieving the objective of living a long life is not sufficient. Quality of life assumes primary concern. How enjoyable can old age be if one suffers from some chronic ailment or one cannot pursue a favorite pastime? With advances in medical care, technology, and an enhanced awareness of healthier lifestyles, people have set the bar higher—life should be healthy, enjoyable, and comfortable.

Some countries have started to promote programs and advisories in an effort to help their senior citizens live happier lives. Just the other week I happened to observe a shuttle bus transporting seniors, some requiring wheelchairs, to a recreation center where they engaged in group activities, including some form of exercise, games, and music. It was a government-sponsored activity. On other occasions, I have seen a group of seniors performing tai chi in slow, intentional movements. Of course, this latter situation pertains to an Asian context. And in this case, I believe the participants took the initiative to organize it as a regular community event. The government is involved by encouraging citizens to stay active, physically and socially. Billy Ray Cyrus's hit "Achy Breaky Heart" may have spawned something comparable in America when his song helped popularize western line dancing. Dancers of all ages may participate. Age is not a deterrent. Skill likewise is not really a requirement. The important point is to get out of the home, away from passively existing, and to embrace life in some active manner that includes social interaction. That results in healthier and happier living.

A spiritual aspect emerges for Christians, old and young. How should older Christians view life at this latter stage of life and how should they spend their days? How should one regard and interact with aged Christians? Since most evangelicals regard the Bible as the ultimate authority in matters of faith and practice, turning to Scripture for guidance represents an essential spiritual discipline. A biblical hermeneutics of ageism provides the framework for reading the sacred text beneficially and avoiding some pitfalls of misreading. Established principles help inform the reading and meditation experience. As an initial attempt at developing such a hermeneutics, one needs to explore and experiment beginning with general principles deemed relevant. Some principles appear more generic and not so specific to ageism but are included in order to provide a foundation. Other principles are narrower and more specific to ageism. For example, the community of believers formed in the local church or other gathering represents a collectivistic dynamic. There is interaction between members. Although disciples of Christ are to love one another, is there a more nuanced interchange between believers where age can have a significant role? What does Scripture say about such relationships?

The Bible portrays several people with whom we older readers can readily relate due to their advanced ages. We want to know what significant roles they played in God's overarching plans and objectives. Affirming that they were still strategic despite being old gives us hope that we too may have important roles in the divine scheme. However, we need hermeneutical principles to guide us in examining these characters and to differentiate between what applies only to them and not to us and what aspects of their lives and service to the Lord can serve as models worth emulating today.

Passages that refer to the aged as general comments or teachings offer potentially insightful thoughts and lessons. Most significantly, these biblical statements give us a glimpse of God's perspective. What is the Lord's attitude toward the elderly and what expectations does he have of them? A biblical hermeneutics would caution us as we read about biblical characters and biblical statements referring to old age not to accept anything at face value without first contextualizing the passages historically and redemptively. We want to uncover the presence of universal concepts and principles that can speak to us today. We complement this process by weeding out what proves unique historically, for example, Moses possessing undiminished physical vigor and eyesight at the age of 120. Redemptive contextualization identifies the particular covenant under which a given biblical text operates, thereby affecting interpretation and application. However, we stand on firmer ground when we consider the Wisdom literature. This corpus of sapient pronouncements transcends history in presenting timeless truths and even culture with generalizations about human nature and the condition of fallen humanity. Hence, what was true and applicable back then remains true and equally applicable today. We do not have to contextualize the original setting and to recontextualize for our present situation. The Wisdom literature represents texts that are the easiest and most straightforward to read and to apply. Then whatever truths the wisdom texts convey are unchanging and relevant truths in any culture and at any point in history. Even a statement about a dull ax requiring greater exertion (Eccl 10:10) can easily be converted to a modern equivalent (for example, a dull kitchen knife).

Given the global prevalence of aging, it seems only appropriate to ascertain the attitudes, concerns, characteristics, and customs with respect to the elderly in Asia and the West. Rather than making overly general and simplistic comments that gravitate toward stereotyping, the investigation starting in the next chapter surveys six specific regions and cultures in Asia and the USA. The selection of these regions depended on accessibility for practical reasons. Thus, any observations and conclusions are specific to those people groups. Attempting to generalize to characterize other regions in Asia or in the West would be potentially inaccurate in view of the great diversity of cultures worldwide.

Introduction

However, gathering information from six distinct Asian people groups offers the potential of identifying some traits or patterns common across the board. One distinctive that emerges in surveying Asia highlights the role and importance of the family. Of course, this finding does not imply that Americans attach lesser significance to the family; rather the difference between East and West lies in the relative extent to which the family is involved in a person's life, decisions, and activities. The Asian concept of family often extends beyond the confines of the nuclear family to include extended family members like grandparents, aunts, uncles, and cousins. The common monikers of "uncle" and "auntie" when addressing an older person not family-related suggests a closer bond within Asian society compared to that in America. With the role of the extended family as a foundation, older people have potentially a more active role in their respective families. Hence, the significance of the elderly may actually increase with age.

In preparation for reading this book, I offer brief summaries of the following chapters to provide an overview. In the next chapter, I document surveys and findings by scientific and governmental authorities that substantiate what we suspect from our own experiences—the world's population is aging. According to projections, the challenge of caring for the aged will increase and seriously impact society, industry, and social services over the next few decades. As a consequence, the subject of ageism is quite urgent and even personal to nearly everyone. Most, if not all of us, have a loved one, a neighbor, or acquaintance, who struggle with some aspect of old age, physically, mentally, emotionally, or financially. Hence, the topic of ageism is an urgent one. Then in the following chapter, chapter 2, a biblical hermeneutics of ageism is presented that forms an objective framework by which to read and to apply the Scriptures with regard to the elderly in our midst. We let the text speak to us authoritatively without intentionally or unintentionally altering the message or teaching by our presuppositions or personal agendas. Chapter 3 reviews the hermeneutical principles identified and reduces them to those that specifically address ageism in a precise fashion exegetically and theologically. This winnowing process does not infer that the other principles are not relevant but rather they form more the background or hermeneutical context. Chapter 4 reviews key biblical characters and passages where old age makes an appearance. Here the historical and literary contexts assume a very essential role. The narrative flow and God's plan, purpose, and intervention, in sum the theological aspect,

Introduction

serve as the parameters by which to assess the passage's potential contribution to ageism. Chapter 5 focuses on the Wisdom literature. Because of the universal and timeless nature of this corpus, the need to contextualize becomes minimal. Hence, this section of sacred writings represents a gold mine from which a treasure trove of valuable insights and lessons can be extracted. Finally, chapter 6 presents some concluding thoughts—reviewing the global phenomenon of ageism, encapsulating the key biblical hermeneutical principles identified, highlighting the book of Ecclesiastes as the wisdom writing with the most concentration of references to old age, and offering a final look at the Asian perspective on this phenomenon.

Chapter 1

A Global Phenomenon and Challenge

RECENT TRENDS

In recent years, a number of surveys and studies confirm that the world's population is aging. A United Nations (UN) report presented some eye-opening statistics.[1] Its opening salvo states: "Population ageing is a global phenomenon: Virtually every country in the world is experiencing growth in the size and proportion of older persons in their population. There were 703 million persons aged 65 years or over in the world in 2019. The number of older persons is projected to double to 1.5 billion in 2050."[2] This report defines 65 years of age as the threshold of old age. But that threshold will likely move upward with the increase in life expectancy. The rate of aging is "fastest in Eastern and South-Eastern Asia and Latin America and the Caribbean," where the percentage of older people "almost doubled from 6 per cent in 1990 to 11 per cent in 2019 in Eastern and South-Eastern Asia."[3] Another report substantiates the rapid rise of this older generation, although the estimated numbers differ, and identifies two primary factors causing this increase—declining birth rates and increasing life spans.[4] The changing demographics exert a potentially profound effect on society—health care of senior citizens, handling the inevitable decline in cognitive ability with age, the impact of losing workers due to retirement with the

---

1. United Nations Economic and Social Affairs, "World Population Ageing 2019."
2. United Nations Economic and Social Affairs, "World Population Ageing 2019."
3. United Nations Economic and Social Affairs, "World Population Ageing 2019."
4. ADB Data Library, "Population and Aging in Asia."

attendant attempt to mitigate that loss by increasing the retirement age, and other social services targeting the aged including supporting families having older members.[5] An earlier 2015 UN report gives a fuller description of the impact on the local government and affected society.[6]

A recent article touted Singapore with having the world's longest life expectancy of 84.8 years.[7] But that lofty number is reduced by 10.6 years on average for poor health, resulting in an adjusted expectancy of 74.2 years in relatively good health. Another article, covering only the G7 nations, identified Japan as enjoying the longest life span of 81.1 years for men and 87.1 years for women.[8] The researchers found that the Japanese diet played a critical role in ensuring longevity. These findings point to the importance of quality of life, especially leading a healthy lifestyle, and not simply the total number of years, as a better gauge to measure a country's success in promoting a long life for its citizens.

If we acknowledge these trends, particularly those that locate the fastest growing elderly populations in Asia, and the somewhat arbitrary target date of 2050 toward which the various statistical graphs point, Asian societies have a little less than thirty years to prepare adequately in the areas of health care, prolonging quality of life, and sustaining economic vitality and growth with an aging workforce.

Traditionally for an Asian society, characterized by the Confucianist principle of filial piety, the family has been the expected resource and refuge for sustaining and supporting the aged. But times and lifestyles have changed in recent decades, resulting in a change of attitudes and practices among Asian families that has prompted a more negative regard for filial piety.[9] For example, many Asians migrate from their rural homes to find

---

5. Smith and Majmundar, *Aging in Asia: Findings*, n.p. Australia, for example, advocates integrated care in the attempt to coordinate the various specialists, agencies, and other health care providers to offer a more efficient and cost-effective health care system where the elderly may experience reduced anxiety and better quality of life (Royal Australasian College of Physicians, "Integrated Care"). New Zealand is the other country striving for integrated care. But, as this report acknowledges, both countries still have a way to go in addressing some remaining issues.

6. United Nations Economic and Social Affairs, "World Population Ageing 2015," 18–19.

7. Khalik, "Singaporeans Have World's Longest Life Expectancy."

8. Tsugane, "Why Has Japan Become the World's Most Long-Lived Country," 922. The G7 nations are Canada, France, Germany, Italy, Japan, the UK, and the US.

9. Woo, "Myth of Filial Piety." Globalization is a major factor affecting family attitudes and practices. See Yap et al., "Aging in Asia," 257–67.

work in the cities, leaving behind their children under the care of grandparents. If the elderly caregivers can manage the household and family, then everything works out well. However, should they experience health issues themselves that complicates matters. There has been a shift in care-giving from the family to institutions.[10] Moreover, prolonged separation of parents from their children can potentially lead to dysfunctional families and leave a profound negative impact on the children. These patterns show that, even with legislation by local governments to reinforce filial piety, families may elect not to comply.[11]

VIEWPOINT OF THE AGED

The studies cited in the previous section examine aging from the point of view of researchers. Although they offer helpful insights and urge an appropriate response from civil authorities to a global phenomenon that will have catastrophic consequences if adequate policies and practices are not in place, the viewpoint of the aged themselves should assume an essential role in any discussion on this matter. What do they think and what are their feelings? What concerns or worries occupy them? Are they struggling with depression, anger, loneliness, pain, and even nostalgia? Do they have plans and hopes for their future? Do they expect support and care from their children?

Researchers find a mixed response to that last question. A number of older people do not want to burden their children. They prefer to live independently and strive to maintain the lifestyle with which they are familiar. Or their relationship with their children may be distant and strained, thereby offering little prospect of support from within the family.

---

10. Yap et al., "Aging in Asia," 4.

11. The governments of Singapore, China and Hong Kong have laws and tax incentives (Yap et al., "Aging in Asia," 4). However, long-term care, intergenerational tension, and alternative forms of care by non-family members mitigate the effectiveness of these official measures. Singapore, for example, has the Maintenance of Parents Act that requires children to care for aged parents sixty years of age and above. See Lim, "Maintenance of Parents Act." China has something similar—the Protection of the Rights and Interests of Elderly People, or the Filial Piety Law. See Dong, "Elder Rights in China," 1429–30. Hong Kong features a number of ordinances. See Government of Hong Kong Special Administrative Region, "Residential Care Homes for the Elderly."

Personal Viewpoint

Being 76 years of age, I have a vested interest in this topic. Likely I'm the exception in that I worked full-time until four years ago when the school where I taught elected not to renew my contract. A fortuitous sequence of events permits me to continue working beyond the normal retirement age in Singapore, currently 63 years of age with the possibility of re-employment until 68.[12] Projections call for further increases, the statutory retirement age to 65 and the re-employment age to 70, respectively.[13] Those adjustments, should they come, will not apply to me since I'm already well beyond the projected increases.[14] In recent years, my main objective focuses on maintaining my health, physically, mentally, emotionally, and spiritually. Preparing and teaching my lessons demands mental acuity. I exercise regularly to address my physical condition and to promote my endurance. Interacting with students through consultation and mentoring challenges me spiritually. And my loving wife provides an emotional anchor.

But the inevitable retirement arrived. For a good half year afterwards, I experienced emotional instability as I felt my identity and self-worth slipping away. Who am I? What is my purpose? What will I do? Great uncertainty gripped me. When the next semester started after retirement, I remember telling a former student that I felt as if the train had departed without me. A significant factor causing my destabilization was my status in the country as I held a soon-to-expire work permit justifying my stay. Without a contract, when my permit expired, I had to leave. I was still in good health and wanted to teach. The school was willing for me to continue as an adjunct but only if I acquired a visa. That was the challenge. How do I obtain official permission to stay?

Again, a fortuitous sequence of events led to my staying longer, at least for a couple of years. Thus, I assume the role as an adjunct. Part-time suits me well as I regain a measure of personal significance and structure for my life and, at the same time, exempts me from the normal stress of working full-time. With somewhat declining endurance compared to ten years before, I appreciate the slower pace the new lifestyle affords me. I can still contribute meaningfully to equipping students for future ministry.

---

12. Lim, "Retirement Age in Singapore." Companies can increase the pertinent ages sooner, at their discretion.

13. "Raising of retirement, re-employment ages in 2022."

14. Those increases apply only to citizens and permanent residents. Neither category applies to me.

Later, I hope to extend my work life a little longer as a volunteer, foregoing contractual pay.

At some point, I realize no one will offer me a contract. Organizations want younger people, cognizant of the latest technology, driven, full of energy and ideas, and having a long career ahead that could potentially translate into many years of useful employment. I see this tendency at the school I teach. The administration favors younger professors who can contribute long term. Then in later years, assuming I'm still healthy, what can I do? How will I occupy myself? These issues prompt the writing of this book, where I will explore the concept of old age, its attendant issues, and the possibilities of positioning this phase of life into a vehicle for fruitful service to the Lord and to others.

THE PUBLIC INTEREST IN AGING IN THE WEST

Online communication represents one prominent feature of modern life. Anyone, it seems, can contribute their thoughts and perspectives on life or on any subject that captures their interest. Even though they do not present themselves as experts, their view still provides a glimpse into their convictions, experiences, and viewpoint. In this section, I share a sampling that can be regarded as equivalent to what I might capture should I go out into the streets and interview people at random. They share either directly or indirectly their opinion about aging and old age.

What strikes me forcefully is the frequency with which the topic and concern about aging appears. In a recent three-day period (May 5 to 7, 2023), the following entries crop up in Quora, an American blogging platform: "What do people who retire really early actually end up doing?" "Do you consider age 60 in the upper range of middle age or the early range of senior?" "How can old age challenges be tackled?" "What is a perfectly balanced diet for a senior citizen?" "What is something that almost nobody knows about retiring early?" Presuming these to be serious, honest questions, we find a growing number of people preoccupied with this subject.

Scott D. Wilson asks "When do you start 'growing old'?

> How do I know when I have started growing old? The minute you stop living. Mark Twain famously said "Most men are dead at 27, we just bury them at 72." Why? Because they stop living and just continue existing. They live simply to work. This is why so many die a few years after retirement.

> Children LIVE! They naturally experience life and anticipate tomorrow. How many adults look avidly forward to the coming years? They see their best years behind them. So they stop living and they grow old.[15]

Mr. Wilson's excerpt equates aging with merely existing, letting time slip by heedlessly, and not living life fully. Such existence does not know about enjoying life, whether spent pursuing a favorite pastime or social engagement with family and friends. There is no sense of adventure or excitement in striving toward a new venture, exploring a new place, or learning new skills as illustrated in the following entry.

Richard Strachan, on That's So Interesting, says:

> Happy 102nd birthday to Agnes Keleti, the world's oldest living Olympic champion! The Holocaust survivor from Hungary won a total of ten gymnastics medals, including five golds, in 1952 and 1956. Today, the energetic centenarian prefers to look forward, asserting: "The past? Let's talk about the future. That's what should be beautiful. The past is past but there is still a future."[16]

Ms. Keleti enjoys a long life marked by noteworthy highlights. But she prefers to look forward, stating: "The past? Let's talk about the future." This perspective can characterize us all who have entered the proverbial "old age." Instead of viewing most of our lives as behind us with very little in front of us, we should anticipate the future as something beautiful into which we can plunge wholeheartedly. Excitement builds, the sense of new adventure prompts us to look forward, not backward. This mindset, I believe, honors the Lord. Paul writes (2 Cor 4:16–17): "Therefore we do not lose heart, but though our outer person is decaying, yet our inner person is being renewed day by day. For our momentary, light affliction is producing for us an eternal weight of glory far beyond all comparison."

Stacia Lucki Roesler, an executive at a major software company, wrote about her father:

> On his 90th birthday I asked "Dad, don't you wish you were 21 again?" His reply was the wisdom of the ages. He said "No, I want to be 60 again. Those were the best years of my life. I was retired and fit and had financial freedom; all my friends were still alive.

---

15. August 1, 2022. https://qr.ae/pKzoM8.
16. January 11, 2023. https://qr.ae/prZLgT.

A Global Phenomenon and Challenge

In my 20s I had no money and still so much toil and worry and heartache ahead of me."[17]

Some forethought confirms the wisdom of Stacia's father. He discovered that the best years followed his retirement, while still physically healthy and financially sound and with friends to enjoy. Even though many see their twenties as being the prime of life, Stacia's father thought otherwise. That early decade of life was marked by too much uncertainty and financial instability. And late in life, after the passing of all his friends, he faced loneliness.

Reflecting on my own journey, I agree about the uncertainty and worry that marked life in my twenties. Engaged in theological education in my sixties, life was much more stable and enjoyable doing what I passionately believed in. Because I relocated to the other side of the world, I left all that was familiar to encounter everything new and somewhat uncertain initially. But a few semesters in, I gained traction and new friends. Now in my seventies, I'm taking life one year at a time. So far, I have lost a couple friends and colleagues, old or new. No doubt, the time will come when many more will pass on. Will I reach 90? Don't know. But I'm not preoccupied with that thought. Just focus on the present and making the most of it.

Cyndi Perlman Fink asks a very disturbing question: "Are old people a burden to society?" This concern may not be the biggest issue we older folks face but it is certainly close to the top of our list. Although Ms. Fink is 74, she writes:

> I don't feel like a burden to society quite yet. I was rushing around the house doing laundry, making the bed, cleaning the kitchen, getting dressed to go out. I asked my husband, who was helping me do several of these things, if he thought there would ever be a day when we would need help doing all this. He said, yes.

She then continues: "I don't want to live into being a burden. I want to go on my own terms. If I don't have a mind, if I can't walk, if I can't talk, if I can't continue to contribute to society, I want out."[18]

We don't want to burden our children and family. We don't want to become a burdensome ward of a hospice, requiring round-the-clock care. I remember visiting my father at an elderly care facility. The staff were professional and pleasant. The services and facilities were adequate and relatively

---

17. 2019. https://qr.ae/pvLztP.
18. 2018. https://qr.ae/pr1USg.

comfortable. They respected my father and the other residents, striving to preserve their dignity. But I struggled to reconcile my image of a younger version of my father when I was a youth with him at the hospice. He was very independent, so much so that, whereas other households called for a technician to fix a broken appliance or the mechanic to repair the car, my father insisted on doing the work himself. He was very handy and quite successful in keeping our home operational. But seeing him being served his meals, helping him clean his room, and assisting him as he walked about, especially outdoors, grieved me. I think his declining physical abilities irritated and even angered him. He lost his independence. A proud man, he did not like being helped.

I saw in my father my own future. Someday I too will need help and become a burden. Will my dignity remain intact when my independence deteriorates? Likely, I too will become irritated at losing my physical functionality and independence. What exacerbated his condition was that my father retained clarity in mental cognition and so was acutely aware of his decreasing mobility.

Another Quora contributor, Donna Ashworth, codified her life-lessons-learnt about aging in "10 Things Time Has Taught Me."

She offers practical advice. I highlight two. One point states: "Your health is obviously important but stress, fear and worry are far more damaging than any delicious food or drink you may deny yourself. Happiness and peace are the best medicine." The emotions and inner peace and tranquility represent important factors to good health and quality of life. Learn to manage negative thoughts and concerns and to focus on the positive. But what lies beyond our control, we must let go and, for those of us trusting in a sovereign God, we give our problems to the Lord and trust that he will intervene.

Another point highlights: "Who will remember you and for what, become important factors as you age. Your love and your wisdom will live on far longer than any material thing you can pass down. Tell your stories, they can travel farther than you can imagine." This point deals with our legacy, what we pass on to others so that they may remember us with gratitude after we are gone; but, more importantly, they will be better off because of what we give to them.[19]

An unknown author once reflected (abridged version):

---

19. 2023. https://qr.ae/pry5mn.

A Global Phenomenon and Challenge

> What does it feel like to be old? After reflection, I concluded that getting old is a gift. I have seen some dear friends leave this world, before they had enjoyed the freedom that comes with growing old. It is true that through the years my heart has ached for the loss of a loved one. But it is suffering that gives us strength and makes us grow.
>
> To answer the question: I like being old, because old age makes me wiser, freer! I know I'm not going to live forever, but while I'm here, I'm going to live by my own laws, those of my heart. The time that remains, I will simply love life as I did, the rest I leave to God.[20]

The perspective of regarding old age as a gift values the experiences and wisdom gained over the years. Suffering is a tough but appreciated teacher that prompts the maturing process—grief over the loss of loved ones. The writer identifies the most valuable gift of all, the freedom to pursue life according to one's convictions, unencumbered by the expectations of others. As idealistic and attractive as that sounds, this particular viewpoint is quite individualistic. Growing up and living in a collectivistic society, one sees such freedom as foreign, even irresponsible to one's family or group. One's noblest ambition strives to honor the social structures that provide identity and the sense of belonging. Whether one's allegiance is to parents, the elders of one's community, or accepted social norms, freedom is the choice to fulfill one's duty for the common good of others.

But evaluating the relative merits of an individualistic and collectivistic mindset goes beyond the confines of this current investigation. Each viewpoint and its attendant choices and practices can result in a full life, if lived to old age. The question becomes: Regardless of viewpoint, will the person experience satisfaction and perhaps a sense of completion in the end?

Concluding Thoughts on the Public Interest in Aging

Each of the selected entries contributes an important insight worthy of our continued reflection and possible application. The contributors share from personal experience or that of people they know well, typically a parent. The number of entries reveals how significant the subject of aging is to many people. Although the blogs originate in the USA, the aging trend

---

20. 2023. https://qr.ae/prY5uR.

globally makes this concern universal. The common trait of these stories is the high regard for the latter portion of life and the desire to live all of life as fully as possible. For the aged, priority focuses on the present and the future rather than on the past. Despite the loss and grief of loved ones by those who outlive their contemporaries and the reduction of energy and even health, hope still resides in their hearts as they look forward to the future, regardless of how much or little time remains.

ASIAN PERSPECTIVE ON AGING

The selected views expressed in the preceding section, taken from Quora, approximate what can be obtained through interviewing people on the streets. In this section, I hope to capture the Asian perspective as well, thereby acquiring a more global representation. In order to accomplish this endeavor, I contacted respondents in Singapore, Malaysia, Thailand, Myanmar, Nagaland (a northeastern state of India), and the Philippines. It is a limited sampling given the great diversity of cultures, languages, and history throughout the vast region that is Asia. For practical reasons, I am only able to communicate with these people. Beforehand, I expected the responses to feature some common ground and also differences with the West and with each other scattered in different Asian regions.

Singapore

Since I am stationed in Singapore, a large portion of my data comes from that region. The respondents range in age from 62 to 70+, relatively young, but most have retired and are not working. Generally, they have a positive view on retirement, seeing this phase as time to enjoy the fruits of their labor, according to one person. Several others view it as an opportunity to reflect on life and to draw closer to God free from the stress of the corporate world. One still working fears the loss of identity and usefulness upon retirement; but this concern is only a projection about the future and does not stem from an actual situation. The definition of old age proves somewhat elusive—one sees it as only a number, rather arbitrary, and another defines it as when the body no longer functions as before, having slowed down and aches and injury take longer to mend. For those who give an actual age, the low end is 65 and the high end is 80+. All agree that health is the primary criterion whereby the loss of well-being signals the onset of old age.

A Global Phenomenon and Challenge

One respondent provides a useful table to contrast the advantages and disadvantages of old age:

Advantages	Disadvantages
1. More opportunity to get a seat on public transport.	1. Be deemed by young people as "useless" to society, or worst "parasite."
2. More likely of respect/honor.	2. Generally, most society associates old peoples with "unhygienic."
3. Some Middle Eastern societies may deem them as "wise" and experienced.	3. Often finds great difficulty to catch up with the fast pace of the digital advancement of today.
	4. Out of sight, thus can be forgotten by others.
	5. Not be able to drive after 75 years old (Singapore).
	6. Loss of the normal physical/mental strength of one's youth.
	7. Care for old people can be a burden to families.

The first advantage sees a greater chance of sitting on public transport, particularly on a train. Often passengers offer their seat to an elderly passenger if none are available. Another advantage typical of Singapore is senior discounts by stores and attractions (for example, amusement venues). In fact, the country offers three kinds of such discounts—first, regular senior discounts for those 60+; second, the Merdeka (Malay for "freedom/independent") generation package offers subsidized health care for those born in the 1950s; and finally, pioneer, for the generation who were at least 16 years of age in 1965 as they constituted the workforce that built the nation.

One disadvantage noted takes the form of reduced income and inadequate pension forcing the retiree to continue working. Slaving away at hawker centers, very old workers clean tables and remove used dishes, cups, and trays. Some are nearly doubled over in posture. As I observe them, I wonder how they get through what for them must be exhausting work.

Some of those trays are heavily ladened. They cannot be enjoying life at this point; and that is sad.

The Singapore government's policy calls for senior citizens to take care of their health through self-care, a healthy lifestyle, and exercise as the first line of defense against the encroachment of old age as there are a number of government-sponsored active care centers. The second line comes from the family that supports a heathy multi-generational environment. A third line comes from social workers. The government's overall objective is to keep the budget for senior health care to a minimum. Consistent with that initiative, active aging centers help to "build strong social connections, take part in recreational activities, and contribute to the community."[21] Seniors may volunteer to visit and befriend homebound seniors, for example, as part of their involvement in this effort.

One senior Singaporean shares:

> We take old age to be an expected time to wind down and to spend more time with family and friends. Everyone is happy that such a one is able to travel if healthy and be satisfied with his/her last days before immobility sets in. For my generation, it is expected for us to at least have some savings to cater for our own care and not to depend on our children. I would love to be able to stay with my children when immobile where I can pay from my own pocket a maid to tend to my needs but am also open to be placed in a nursing home should my medical condition becomes a greater burden to them.

I offer a few observations based on his sharing. One, workers are required to have the mandatory Central Provident Fund (CPF), a social security savings scheme.[22] Two, they want some financial independence so as not to overly burden their families. Three, employing maids or domestic help is a common practice. Four, there exists facilities for intensive care should the elderly become incapacitated.

Everyone interviewed agrees that health is the number one determinant for quality of life. If struggling with an illness or some debilitating condition, the elderly cannot enjoy life, socialize, volunteer, pursue fulfilling activities, or even care for their grandchildren. They become a burden to their families or to society.

---

21. Agency for Integrated Care, "Active Ageing Centres."
22. Ministry of Manpower, "Central Provident Fund."

Malaysia

Generally, the younger generation has a high regard for old people (60+). They are highly respected for their wisdom and insights into their culture and religion. Because of their Islamic beliefs, they strive to impart cultural values and insights and religious practices to their children and grandchildren. Because of strong family bonding, the younger generation look to the elderly for parental advice and guidance, especially with regards to tradition and faith. Malays believe that caring for their aged parents is a religious obligation. Even if the younger people move to the cities to live and work, they still maintain close ties with their family in the rural villages. They make every effort to return to see their elderly relatives as often as they can. They value those relationships.

Nowadays, the older generation seem hesitant to get directly involved in their children or grandchildren's lives, unless they deem it necessary. They let the young people choose their careers and life partners. And if a young couple opts for a Western style wedding in lieu of a traditional Malay wedding, the older generation will accept their decision.

A recent trend, however, reveals the increase in broken families, divorces, and the elderly being sent to old folks homes. Several factors may explain this disturbing pattern—higher cost of living, major differences in opinion, the subtle encroachment of Western culture, and the more open-minded thinking of the young people.

Thailand

Thais honor their parents and the elderly generally. However, the young people may not regard old people as a source of wisdom or seek their advice. The avowed respect is more in principle rather than in practice. Theirs is a remote respect. When the children leave the village to find work in the city, they leave their own children in the care of the grandparents. They send money back to support their aged parents.

Interestingly, a discernable difference separates Thai Chinese and Thai Thais. The former group exhibits a stronger connection with the elderly. The older generation has a more active role as a sought-after source of advice and opinions because their wisdom comes from experience. Thai Thais, however, manifest a looser relationship. Parents give their children the freedom to make their own decisions without the need to consult with them.

As an example, an older woman's daughter works in Bangkok, quite a distance from her rural home. Frequently, her daughter sends parcels of food and snacks. Several times a year, her daughter visits. This pattern is very common in separated families. The ties remain strong even if distant.

Myanmar

A retiree from the Kachin tribe living in northern Myanmar shares her thoughts on the cultural aspects of the elderly:

> Kachin culture sees those with "grey hair" as the symbol of peace and unity of a community and the character of a prosperous community, for where there are elders, there are young people. This old-age and young-age relationship assures prosperity. In addition to childcare support, elders are sought after for wisdom and knowledge. They are valuable counselors and sources of wisdom. They are the history and have the wisdom to see the future. Young people are wise to consult the elders' knowledge and lived experience on approaching life wisely, which is something their peers cannot offer.

The elderly have symbolic value. They symbolize wisdom and knowledge accumulated from a long life of experiences and observations. They assure the continued prosperity of the community where the old and young live together in harmony. This respondent notes the strategic value of old people—they remember the past, the history of the people; they bless the present generation with their collective wisdom; and they can forecast the future based on discerned patterns and trends.

Nagaland

In his sixties, a Naga man still working offers his perspective based on the culture of his people:

> In the Naga culture, the primary concern of older people relates to their children's and grandchildren's well-being regarding marrying them off ("matchmaking") to build a family. Also, they take their role of caring for their grandchildren seriously and do so passionately; as a result, the grandparents-grandchildren bond is

strong. Sometimes stronger than the parent-children bond. This is possible within the traditional extended family of different generations, unlike the modern practice of burdening the grandparents with raising their grandchildren alone.

Very strong family bonds across three generations characterize the nuclear family. The elderly often assumes the primary responsibility of raising the grandchildren. Interestingly, the relationship between grandparent and grandchild may be stronger than that with the children, the parents of the grandchild. I find this dynamic to be the case also for one Singaporean retiree who enjoys a very close relationship with his grandchildren now that he has time to interact with them. But when he was working, he rarely returned home early enough to see his children before their bedtime. Consequently, his relationship with them is currently strained.

The Naga respondent provides a distinctive cultural practice as he narrates:

> Unlike the biblical practice of inheriting the family wealth by the firstborn son, in Naga culture, the lastborn receives the inheritance, including the responsibility of caring for aging parents but done so sincerely and naturally due to the stronger bond between the youngest and the parents.

Logically the practice makes sense. The child enjoying the strongest bond with the parents would naturally be more inclined to care for them, although in other cultures the firstborn receives preferential treatment, especially the male child.

Interestingly, none of the respondents indicate that gender plays an influential role in the family. Historically, China, for example, shows a profound preference for sons over daughters.[23] Perhaps that omission is due to the focus on the elderly rather than the children or grandchildren. The impression from their sharing suggests that offspring, male or female, are all precious.

Philippines

In Filipino culture, the elderly (60+) are deeply respected. Their families insist that they live with and provide for them. Consequently, retirement homes, senior homes, or hospices seem practically nonexistent. Families

---

23. Wang et al., "Son Preference and Reproductive Behavior."

tend to be multi-generational. Grandparents not only represent a source of experience and wisdom, but their blessing and decision-making are keenly sought after. Although everyone in the family may offer input on an issue, often the grandparent(s) have the final say. When celebrating a special event, the family ensures that the elderly have a place of honor at the table and are served. If some family members live overseas, they make the effort to commemorate their grandparent's birthday in person. Thus, the elderly possess great honor and assume a position of prominence within the family. They also enjoy discounts at stores, restaurants, utilities, public transportation, and medicine, even benefiting from tax exemption. They circumvent long queues.

THOUGHTS ON THE ASIAN PERSPECTIVE

The observation that various physical and mental challenges accompany the onset of old age is universal, across cultures. We may recall our younger years with some nostalgia but must grapple with our present reality. Another shared view sees continued good health as the primary contributor to quality of life. Age may be just a number but health or the lack of it can rob one of functionality, joy, and contentment regardless of age.

Among Asians, the family proves quite central. This does not imply that in the West family concerns have no importance; but it is clearer in Asia. Unlike individualistic cultures where the older person envisions travel, embarking on some new adventure or pursuing some personal dream upon retirement, collectivistic cultures tend to focus more on family relationships, particularly those between grandparents and grandchildren. Before retirement work commitments leave parents little energy for and time with their children. But with retirement, their lives free up significantly and they fill in the gap for their children who are now busy working in caring for their grandchildren. Indeed, several respondents admit to a closer relationship with grandchildren than with their own children. This dynamic provides the opportunity to bless the younger generation with the wisdom and experience accumulated over a lifetime. They assume the respected role of teacher, advisor, story-teller, and even playmate. They personify the teacher or mentor in Proverbs.

The elderly desire some financial independence in order not to burden their families. They want the freedom to live on their own or have some responsibility within the extended family and not simply be recipients of care and support. This lifestyle preserves their dignity. Quite a few Western blogs espouse self-care routines in order to maintain health and quality of life. Whereas these insights are useful, Asians give more emphasis on meeting the needs of others, particularly younger family members in their formative years. This focus provides a clear purpose of investing in young lives, thereby perpetuating a legacy that will offer continuing dividends in the years ahead, long after one's life is but a memory—a beloved memory.

An important Asian distinction emerges—the attribute of honor and esteem takes precedence over love or being loved, not that the latter is absent. The family deeply respects the elderly and, to some degree, derive their honor or reputation from their elders. In Filipino culture, the younger generation bestow various honorific titles on the elderly, being careful not to call them by first name only. Because of our close bond, two former students address me as *ninong* ("godfather") and my wife as *ninang* ("godmother") because we are their godparents. Sometimes they include my name with the title, and so I am called "*ninong* Gilbert." Our relationship is bidirectional, where I show care and concern for their well-being although we are separated by an ocean. This relational dynamic in Asian cultures helps explain the critical truth behind the biblical admonitions to heed a father's instruction (for example, Prov 1:8; 4:1). The context of the passages cited regard the teachable child as "wise" (Prov 1:1–7, 20–23 and 4:2–13). The compatible expression would be a "respectful" child in Asia. Obviously, in order for the young to accept the elderly's teaching, they must respect the elder so that wisdom may pass down from one generation to the next. Respect values the experience and wisdom of the old.

As a reflection of the diversity in Asia, culturally and religiously, my survey of six regions reveals some differences in the attitude toward the elderly. The strongest bond between the generations appears to be in the Philippines and the least among Thai Thais. Of course, I do not imply that this latter group shows no respect for old people; the observation is relative. Malaysia offers the clearest example of how religious beliefs affect the generational bond. A common phenomenon is work migration where young people move away to find employment, creating separation from their parents and, in some cases, from their own children.

The differences between Asia and the West may be due, to a significant degree, to the differences between a collectivist versus an individualist society. Other studies have already confirmed this observation.

THE CHRISTIAN SCRIPTURAL VIEWPOINT

A second motivation for writing this book is the desire to bring Scripture and its perspective on this important topic front and center. In the heading above, I explicitly mention "Christian" in order to distinguish my findings below from the sacred writings of other faiths (for example, Islam). I view it as God's word and authoritative. It should inform our thoughts, viewpoint, and feelings—we humans are both rational and emotional beings. In order to safeguard our reading of the Bible so that we do not proof text or uncritically apply the text, we will devote the next chapter to the biblical hermeneutics of ageism. Normally, we approach the Bible with an open mind and heart, eager to discern God's voice through our reading. We don't bring a personal agenda that might color whatever insights we may extract. A common error is seeing something in the text—justification for our favored stance on some issue or a specific message about a pressing personal dilemma—because we are convinced of its validity beforehand. Is what we see really in the text or is it a mirage of our imagination? On the other hand, none of us can come to the Bible completely open, without presuppositions. We may mitigate potential bias, however, if we are aware of our own inclinations and assumptions and apply a rigorous self-check to ensure that we have sufficient evidence to support our position. Whether our interpretation of the text is correct depends on the principles that we use.

Passage selection for investigation plays an important role that can have a big impact on any conclusions we draw from the text. Unsurprisingly, passages that feature age, either of the character in question or of the import of the text, represent candidates for examination. The simple record of a character's age, for example, the age of kings and the length of their reign in the Kings and Chronicles books, may not be viable candidates for study, however. In particular, we look for references to old age and its role and significance in the narrative. The distance historically and culturally between the ancient past and present-day complicates matters.[24] The stories of the aged in the ancient world cannot be correlated to today's situations and challenges older people face in a straightforward manner. There has to be some kind of bridging between the two worlds. In the chapter on the

---

24. Carson labels this phenomenon "distanciation" (*Exegetical Fallacies*, 127–29). He also discusses "historical fallacies," the speculative filling in the gaps of the biblical narrative that then becomes the basis for overly confident and even dogmatic reconstruction of history (*Exegetical Fallacies*, 131–33). Fee and Stuart offer a related treatment on cultural relativity (*How to Read the Bible*, 80–86).

WHAT IS OLD AGE?

"What is old age?" is a deceptively simple question that leads to not so simple answers. A plethora of responses come from different quarters. In an interesting article, Pinsker struggles to find an acceptable term for those considered old.[25] After presenting a number of suggested terms, he settles on "older" as being the least offensive, although it is not without issues also. But the numerical threshold for old age varies with different points of view, whether it's 60 and above, mid-seventies, or 80+. Some suggest the retirement years, but not everyone retires as some older people continue working while their peers retire. Pinsker concludes his piece by citing another writer with what he considers an elegant definition of old age: "What I think of as old is an age when you start seeing people you know in the obituary column. I think of middle age as a time when you're not afraid to look at the obituaries, because you assume that the people who have died you're not going to know."[26] This particular definition identifies death as the indelible demarcation of old age. But if many people dislike being called "old," then they will find the specter of death even more distressing. Let's face it—who wants to occupy their waking hours thinking about death, either their own or that of others they know?

A recent World Health Organization report states that the number of older people will nearly double by 2050.[27] More people will live beyond 60 than ever before. But, as the report emphasizes, the key to living well in the later years depends on one's health—not just physical well-being but one's mental and emotional health plays a crucial role. Hence, quality of life provides a measure of how well an older person enjoys life and pursues personal significance. Another study evaluates a person's morbidity, depending on whether they suffer from a disability or not in their later years of life.[28] Thus, the important issue does not center on the length of

---

25. Pinsker, "When Does Someone Become 'Old'?"
26. Pinsker, "When Does Someone Become 'Old'?"
27. World Health Organization, "Ageing and Health."
28. Leveille et al., "Aging Successfully until Death," 654–64.

one's life but the quality of life and relative health one continues to enjoy as they enter the later years.

A PERSONAL EXPERIENCE WITH RETIREMENT

As I mentioned earlier, I experienced an emotional upheaval when I ceased working full-time. The institution for which I taught full time decided it was time not to renew my contract by not renewing my employment visa since I was a foreigner working overseas. Even though they had extended my employment beyond the normal age of retirement by a number of years, for which I was extremely grateful, I still harbored mixed emotions tending more toward the negative ones. Positively, I would no longer need to attend meetings or to handle administrative duties and the occasional "other responsibilities as assigned." But negatively, I felt like a boat adrift without a rudder. I lost my bearings with no hard objective to pursue. Surprisingly, I also sensed that my identity and self-worth were shaken to the point where I experienced difficulty sleeping restfully or sleeping at all. It was something I did not expect as I did not realize how closely I tied my occupation with my identity.

I believed and hoped that I could continue working regardless of age so long as I was physically and mentally functional. On a few occasions, I expressed to colleagues my desire to teach my very last class after which the Lord immediately calls me home. So I never planned for nor wanted retirement. But, alas, life does not cooperate.

I recall a friend who, upon retirement, gleefully spent his days on the golf course. However, I cannot relate to him and his euphoria. For one thing, I do not play golf nor can I see myself on the golf course, all day, every day, for the years ahead. Of course, if I am part of the PGA Tour making millions, that would be different. Then doing eighteen holes would be like going to the office and getting compensated with a fat paycheck (assuming I place high in the leader board).

Now several years into my "retirement" I continue with meaningful ministry. I teach as an adjunct and occasionally speak in local churches. My missions organization imposes no age limit after which I must step down. Thus, I've managed to extend my career at least a little longer. At some point, however, I know the opportunities will evaporate as schools want younger faculty with much of their careers before them to bring fresh ideas and high energy. Admittedly, my energy level and endurance have diminished somewhat over the years and represent the inevitable signs of aging. And should the medically enhanced life expectancy grant me more years, what then? How then shall I live presuming decent health?

Most of my peers happily occupy themselves with grandchildren. A few of them have become, in my words, "professional grandparents." Extended family offers potentially rich and rewarding life-experiences in later life. But, in my case, my children are very career-minded and have not given me grandchildren. So I must seek other avenues to ensure quality of life. For example, the present project on the twilight years occupies my time meaningfully in which I have a personal stake.

ACTIVE LIFESTYLE

I have two personal observations about older people spending their twilight years meaningfully. First, a number of older men and women pursue the healthy lifestyle through physical activity to varying degrees of intensity. In fact, a 78-year-old grandmother competed in a powerlifting event and lifted 245 pounds (111.13 kilograms) off the ground.[29] She achieved this impressive feat after working out twice a week at a local gym for two years. Even more impressive is the news about a 97-year-old grandmother who developed a passion for powerlifting over the course of six years, visiting the gym three times a week and competing six times a year.[30] Before we dismiss those two older women as the exception, however, a scientific study covering thirteen thousand adults concluded that regular resistance exercise (for example, weightlifting) totaling less than one hour a week can "reduce the risk of heart attack or stroke by 40% to 70%."[31] The article states that any weightbearing activity may provide similar benefits, such as carrying heavy groceries. Health benefits from such exercises include reducing cardiovascular disease risk as well as enhancing bone health and general quality of life. Of course, jogging and other cardio exercises can greatly improve one's well-being, physically and emotionally. The important factor is pursuing an active lifestyle with some form of physical activity, whether exercise or other physical exertion.

Personally, I used to go to a gym for regular exercise before the advent of COVID-19 that closed gyms across the board for a time and then

---

29. *Good News Network*, "78-year-old Grandmother Powerlifting 245 Pounds."
30. *Express Digest*, "97-Year-Old Grandmother Competitive Weightlifter."
31. Renner, "Study: Little Weight Lifting."

reopened. Because gyms had been identified as potential hotspots to get infected, I avoid going and, instead, have opted to do calisthenics at an outdoor playground equipped with pull-up and parallel bars and the like. Of course, exercising outdoors provides fresh air and sunshine but also rain that can make it challenging.

A second observation I have made focuses on the example of local hawker centers, a unique feature of Singapore where I live and work. These semi-outdoor eateries feature a good number of older clienteles, who appear to be retirees, spending their time there daily, often in groups. As regulars, they chat among themselves, forming an informal social gathering. They eat and drink but, it appears, their primary purpose is to interact with one another. They spend a good portion of each day there. They seem to have their own tables and the servers know them well. Such social interaction is an essential healthy practice, fostering a sense of belonging to a community, supplementing the family unit. This results in emotional and mental health.

Each locality offers its own opportunities to engage in community, fostering social interaction and, if it's a faith gathering, spiritual interaction may also be possible and even desirable.

Should these two lifestyle choices characterize a person, they may be able to delay the onset of some of the negative traits of old age. Their physical, mental, emotional, and even spiritual well-being can carry far into the later years accompanied with a positive outlook on life and the future.

Chapter 2

Biblical Hermeneutics of Ageism

This set of suggested hermeneutical principles and ideas for reading and interpreting Scripture is a first attempt at guiding an older reader (rather subjective descriptive as each person may differ in their self-assessment as to their age and stage in life) in their approach of the text and perception of it addressing them personally. This attempt does not represent a negative criticism of traditional hermeneutics that does not factor in the age of the reader but seeks a sensitive and possibly more nuanced reading. It is assumed that many readers would not be besieged by the symptoms of advancing age (for example, dulling intellectual faculties, declining physical vigor and strength, and the reduction of involvement in society, including lessening of work responsibilities and activities, possibly retirement). In other words, they are busily pursuing their studies, working, social involvement, and other personal goals of interest.

As a preliminary step, I wish to state three of my presuppositions when approaching the biblical text. First, I affirm that a sovereignly authoritative God is the divine author who has utilized human writers to record his words and thoughts, and so a priority for me is discerning what God says and means and his intentions for saying it. I am not at liberty to use the text to further my own personal agenda. Thus, I try to avoid making the text speak about ageism when, in fact, it does not. There should be a relatively clear textual indication to justify my attempt to do so. Second, I assume the text represents a coherent thread of thought as normal discourse. Then to understand the intended message of a given text I need to consider the literary context—what is stated before and after the subject text, that is, the immediate context, and also the broader context of the rest of the passage to capture the flow of thought that contributes to the major point communicated—in order to interpret properly. Third, I respect the historical and cultural context within which the passage first emerges. The writing is a product of its time. However, I am quite aware that my knowledge of the ancient past features gaps that cannot be filled. I may make assumptions or guesstimates where hard data does not exist. Thus, I remain tentative about some conclusions, especially if based on those assumptions.[1]

In this chapter, I document my evaluations of potential leads that bear on ageism. I record my thought process as I examine key Scripture passages. I strive to let the passage speak without forcing an interpretation alien to the text, recognizing instead the primary message emanating from it. When I find something that appears to offer a promising insight on ageism at the outset but, upon further investigation, I realize that that is not the case, I proceed to draw the proper hermeneutical principle even if it proves too generic and does not contribute specifically to my objective of developing the set of principles on ageism. But I will not forward that principle to the next step where I summarize all the relevant principles uncovered.

SUGGESTED PRINCIPLES AND IDEAS

The following sections identify and discuss the hermeneutical principles.

The Unchanging Character of God and Believers

Given God's unchanging character (Heb 13:8) and his eternal word (Ps 119:160b) being true (Ps 119:160a), readers reflect in a finite way his character as they bear his image (Gen 1:27) and are responsible for obeying his commands, regardless of their stage in life. Then regardless of age, readers respond to Scripture in full obedience, their responsibility to God and his word undiminished. The moral aspect of their personhood remains the same even if other aspects do not (for example, the physical and intellectual aspects suffer from the ravages of aging). Hence, their moral accountability remains unaffected. God fully expects every reader, young, middle aged, or aged, to honor him with reverence and submission.

---

1. Carson criticizes the "uncontrolled historical reconstruction" of those attempting to reconstruct the past based on speculation and then becoming overly dependent on it (*Exegetical Fallacies*, 131–33).

Something of this characterization emerges whenever the text depicts God's people collectively. Regularly addressed as "saints" (Pss 16:3; 34:9; Rom 1:7; 8:27; 15:31; 1 Cor 1:2; 6:1–2; Eph 1:1; 2:19; 1 Tim 5:10; Heb 13:24), we do not discern any differentiation into categories within the community of God's people. Then, we may safely assume, unless the text provides a specific mention of subgroups, that God views all members among his people as equally precious, regardless of gender, age, marital status, or even positional status as a leader or simply a member.

A sober reminder that age offers no excuses to slacken morally comes from Moses's warning to Israel, poised to enter the promised land (Deut 4:25–26):

> When you father children and grandchildren, and you grow old in the land, and you act corruptly, and make an idol in the form of anything, and do what is evil in the sight of the Lord your God to provoke him to anger, I call heaven and earth as witnesses against you today, that you will certainly perish quickly from the land where you are going over the Jordan to take possession of it. You will not live long on it, but will be utterly destroyed.

Today, we can claim that the period cited lies in the distant past about another people, culture, and religious milieu. But God's unflinching demand for moral integrity, especially on the part of the elderly, continues to resonate with us. Deuteronomy anticipates Israel's subsequent history in the land by presenting commands and warnings as the people prepare to enter and live a more settled life than their wilderness wanderings. Thus, Moses's final admonitions serve as the standard by which the people are judged throughout OT history even unto Jesus' day.[2] The new covenant that Jesus initiated at the First Advent (1 Cor 11:25) ushers in a new period in salvation history. Yet, the moral demands remain the same as we find through Paul's writings (Titus 2:1–5):

> But as for you, proclaim the things which are fitting for sound doctrine. Older men are to be temperate, dignified, self-controlled, sound in faith, in love, in perseverance. Older women likewise are to be reverent in their behavior, not malicious gossips nor enslaved to much wine, teaching what is good, so that they may encourage the young women to love their husbands, to love their children,

---

2. See, for example, Swanepoel, "Important Function of Deuteronomy," 375–88. Also, Craigie, *Book of Deuteronomy*, 36–45. Historically, Moses renews the covenant that defines the relationship between God and Israel going forward.

to be sensible, pure, workers at home, kind, being subject to their own husbands, so that the word of God will not be dishonored.

The honor accorded the word of God depends, in part, on the lifestyle and life choices of older men and women. Paul's instructions conform to sound doctrine. Then, perhaps, *we may describe the hermeneutic principle of covenantal stipulations as an enduring divine mandate on God's people, including the aged, spanning much of history, the covenants with Abraham and Moses to the new covenant that demand our contemporary stewardship.* Moral principles remain an unwavering constant, based on God's unchanging moral character. No member of the covenant community ever grows so old as to find their membership expiring. They continue as part of the community until death. Thus, their covenantal responsibilities remain in full force. Age does not excuse them from accountability to the Lord. Then we have *an important corollary: read Scripture as everyone else regardless of age or station in life unless the text clearly specifies an age-specific admonition.*

Explicit in Moses's admonition and Paul's is the influence of the older generation on the younger generation. Of special note, fathers have a powerful impact on their children and grandchildren. Older church members can encourage younger members to follow their personal piety and heed their instructions. More on this aspect will be discussed later.

Universal Accountability Requires Wisdom

Warnings against unfaithfulness to the Lord and the resultant consequences apply to everyone, young and old, male or female, married or single. Moses's song, for example, captures the comprehensiveness of the warnings (Deut 32:23, 25): "I will add misfortunes to them; I will use up my arrows on them. Outside the sword will make them childless, and inside, terror—both young man and virgin, the nursing child with the man of gray hair." Although we can argue that a nursing child has not reached the age of accountability, historically Moses addresses the people collectively. If judgmental disaster occurs, it impacts everyone indiscriminately. The aged are as capable of evil and provoking the Lord's displeasure as the young (Deut 4:25–28).

The only appreciable difference experienced by God's people is the personal guilt of each individual and the seriousness of their transgression. Ezekiel 18 provides a lengthy treatment on the accountability of each individual, righteous or wicked, before the Lord. A father does not assume the son's guilt and vice versa. A son cannot blame his father for being a bad example as an excuse for his own conduct. Even if his father commits evil, he can choose to do right before the Lord. He affirms that his judgment of everyone is just (Ezek 18:24–29; a shorter version appears in Jer 31:29–30).

We may question the applicability of this OT portrait of God and his manner of accountability by claiming a disjunction between the OT and the NT. The crux of the matter lies in the continued relevance of the Law for today. Are we to observe the Law in the age of grace? Does not Paul advocate that the good news highlights faith in God's grace as the path toward justification (Rom 3:21–26; Gal 2:15–16)? Then pursuing the works of the Law makes no one righteous before God. But faith has always been the operating principle even in OT times as the chapter recording the OT saints renowned for faith make clear (Heb 11).

The laws of Moses can be categorized into three kinds—the moral, civil, and ceremonial laws.[3] Of the three, only the moral law continues to demand observance today. As one writer notes: "First, the moral law states God's principles for a right relationship with him and with others. The Ten Commandments are the most visible and powerful expression of God's will for his people. As we read the New Testament and reflect on the Bible as a whole, we see that these commands are still operative."[4] The Ten Commandments encode general moral principles and give rise to the various examples of case law (for example, Lev 19:19 states: "You are to keep my statutes. You shall not cross-breed two kinds of your cattle; you shall not sow your field with two kinds of seed, nor wear a garment of two kinds of material mixed together.") that are specific applications of the general moral principles. These applications reflect the cultural and historical milieu of the Israelites and so are not directly applicable today.[5]

The moral law, expressing God's command to his people, remains operative, transcending the particular culture and historical-redemptive

---

3. Bayes traces the history of recognizing the threefold division of the Law to Augustine and even earlier and affirms that the division is scriptural ("Threefold Division of the Law," 3–15).

4. Longman, *Making Sense of the Old Testament*, 110.

5. Longman, *Making Sense of the Old Testament*, 111–23. By cultural differences, citing the examples above, we recognize that most of us living in the twenty-first century do not live in a primarily agricultural society and so will not have the chance to cross-breed animals or plant mixed seed. And by historical differences, we mean our location in salvation history after the First Advent of Christ and the coming of the indwelling Holy Spirit.

situation in which the divine will is first revealed. *In order to obey the moral law, especially as recorded in the OT, we must perform the necessary contextualization to overcome the disjunction between the OT and the NT, and between the ancient and the modern.* The particular case law or circumstance in its original setting points back to a general moral principle that calls for an implementation that may look substantially different in a later setting. Such a practice requires wisdom. Proverbially, the aged are renowned for their wisdom and the younger generation would be wise to tap into that reservoir of knowledge and experience.

Our challenge is to act our age. This is Elihu's expectation of Job's three friends as he declares (Job 32:6b–7): "I am young in years and you are old; therefore I was shy and afraid to tell you what I think. I thought age should speak, and increased years should teach wisdom." Disappointed with these three old men's failure to give an effective rebuttal to Job, however, Elihu then says (Job 32:8–9): "But it is a spirit that is in mankind, and the breath of the Almighty gives them understanding. The abundant in years may not be wise, nor may elders understand justice." He explains that these men should have displayed wisdom given their advanced age but do not and so their shortcomings compel him to speak. He then makes two significant contributions to the dispute between the four: first, suffering may not always be the result of wrongdoing but can be God's means of correcting an erroneous attitude or preventing them from committing a grave error; and second, suffering may showcase God's mercy rather than his wrath.[6] Elihu points out Job's inconsistent reliance on God's justice while, at the same time, questioning that justice given his perceived unwarranted suffering.[7] Elihu's main criticism highlights the four disputants' inadequate theological understanding. The three friends confine God's interaction with humans to retributive justice—he blesses the righteous and punishes sinners. They think that God only acts within that narrow constraint. But having access to the book's first two chapters, we readers know of Job's innocence. Yet, Job himself acts presumptuously in inferring that God unjustly afflicts him.

The kind of wisdom inferred from our reading of Job that older folks should have and display is theological and spiritual;[8] *and we must pass*

6. Hartley, *Job*, 427, 430.
7. Smick, "Job," 4:998.
8. This characteristic is true of the biblical wisdom literature in general and not just for Job. See Murphy, *Tree of Life*, 111–31. Providing an overview on the ancient wisdom literature of Israel and other cultures, Crenshaw notes that, on a practical level, wisdom represents the ability to navigate effectively through the complexities and challenges of

that wisdom on to the next generation so that they too revere the Lord. The younger generation represented by Elihu watch and listen to us closely. Will they be disappointed like Elihu or will they be instructed in better understanding God and his ways in order to live in the world he created because of our wisdom? We must all give an account to the Lord. Wisdom enables us to obtain his approval. But wisdom involves more than knowing and practicing right speech and conduct; it includes an adequate view of God's majesty, sovereign authority, and holiness. It is in his holy and awe-inspiring presence that we pursue life and service. Our perspective of God undergirds our wisdom by which we honor him with our devotion.

The Promises We All Receive, Old and Young

Conversely, the biblical promises of blessing apply to all. The one condition for claiming the promises is fidelity to God and his commandments, as Moses makes clear to Israel as they enter the promised land (Deut 26:16–19). The promises emerge from the covenants God makes with his people or with humanity and all the living as in the covenant with Noah (Gen 9:8–17). God's promise to bless Abraham as the father of many peoples (Gen 12:1–3), reiterated later (Gen 15:1–21; 17:1–22), showcases Abraham's belief in the promise. Much later in the renewal of the covenant with Israel as they stand at the threshold of the promised land, Moses recites the blessings and curses for obedience and disobedience, respectively (Deut 28:1—30:20). The conditional promises depend on their continued submission. To David, God promises an eternal throne, house, and kingdom undergirded by his enduring love (2 Sam 7:4–17). And the new covenant promises internalizing the law and a special relationship between God and his people, and forgiveness of sins (Jer 31:31–34), reiterated and affirmed in the NT (Luke 22:20; 1 Cor 11:25; 2 Cor 3:6; Heb 8:6–13; 9:15; 12:24). We claim the promises of the covenants with Noah, Abraham, and the new. We honor Christ as our king through the Davidic promise.

All God's people, old and young, receive his promises. We all depend on God's faithfulness and truth to preserve his commitments to us. At the same time, we all, old and young, must obey him wholeheartedly. Then his promised blessings are ours to enjoy. The NT rephrases our blessed position as God's children by calling us heirs as Paul proclaims (Rom 8:14–17a):

---

life and relationships (*Old Testament Wisdom*, 4–8).

> For all who are being led by the Spirit of God, these are sons and daughters of God. For you have not received a spirit of slavery leading to fear again, but you have received a spirit of adoption as sons and daughters by which we cry out, "Abba! Father!" The Spirit himself testifies with our spirit that we are children of God, and if children, heirs also, heirs of God and fellow heirs with Christ.

But we ask what principles of interpretation enable us to identify those promises we can claim and which ones we cannot. Perhaps, by taking another perspective, we ask, Which promises can be fulfilled in our lives? Promises, for example, to Israel of rain, land and flock fertility, and safety from surrounding nations upon continued obedience are meant only for the original recipients. Let me propose that *an important hermeneutical principle is to identify all Messianic prophecies fulfilled in Jesus Christ as the most impactful promise we can receive.* These apply to us because he is our Lord and Savior. Christ embodies the ultimate fulfillment of the covenants with Abraham, Moses, David, and the new covenant articulated by Jeremiah. What does Christ mean to us? Paul states it best (1 Cor 1:30–31): "But it is due to him that you are in Christ Jesus, who became to us wisdom from God, and righteousness and sanctification, and redemption, so that, just as it is written: 'Let the one who boasts, boast in the Lord.'" Through Christ we have access to the Father (John 14:6) and to the proffered abundant life (John 10:10). All the goodness of God lies within reach. We pray in Jesus' name, our only mediator with God (1 Tim 2:5; Heb 8:6; 9:15; 12:24). Jesus Christ is the most important promise given by Scripture that we can receive. All other promises are subsumed under that preeminent Messianic promise. We echo Paul's rhetorical question (Rom 8:32): "He who did not spare his own Son, but delivered him over for us all, how will he not also with him freely give us all things?" In Christ we can conquer all things (Rom 8:37). Nothing can separate us from the love of God in Christ Jesus (Rom 8:38–39), not even old age and its attendant challenges whether physical, mental, or emotional. God's love shows no bias—he loves children, young adults, the middle aged, and yes, the old aged. Thus, the specter of death, either of those we know or our own impending end, does not faze us.

The Messianic promises speak to us, affirming our identity as God's children and ensuring us of continued blessings, even as we may struggle with the encroaching infirmities of our age. We continue to hope and even to plan, optimistic in the possibilities for our future, however long or short it may be. The analogy of Israel journeying through the wilderness speaks to our situation as we walk through this time of the aged. The wilderness offers no life-sustaining features to the traveler. They must depend solely on God for their provisions. We too look at our circumstances and likely find less to sustain our vitality compared to earlier years. Our faith in the Lord must prove stronger than ever before. We cling to him and do not give up. As our ancient predecessors have set the example, we follow the Lord's lead believing that he guides us ever closer to the promised land, step by step, day by day. Now is the time to exercise deep, unwavering faith when external evidences of his presence fade with increasing struggles to get through each day. Death is not our fate but his promises are our destiny.

Spiritual Warfare of the Aged

Total reliance on Scripture while engaged in spiritual warfare remains a constant spiritual discipline. No indication in the word of God suggests that the Adversary discriminates based on age. Anyone can be targeted for attack if they suffer a weakness in their armor (Eph 6:10–17). Moral and spiritual vigilance demands continued, unabated alertness (1 Thess 5:1–11). Jesus Christ serves as our model of resisting temptation in his total reliance on the word of God (Matt 4:1–11; Luke 4:1–13). The wilderness represents hostile conditions in which a person encumbered by their vulnerabilities must face the attack in a state of weakness as Jesus in his hunger. If being aged creates a vulnerability, then greater reliance on Scripture must be pursued because the Adversary is ruthless. The aged, then, must pursue the spiritual disciplines of reading and meditating on Scripture and of prayer with greater vigor, knowing full well that the challenges accompanying their stage in life threaten to rob them of the joy in the Lord and the zest for life typifying the young. The specter of impending death casts a pall over various aspects of life because of the news of another friend, associate, or family member dying or the signs of one's own health declining. It can result in gloom and even depression. The Adversary can attack a person in that state of mind. Then *a hermeneutical principle emerges: read and interpret Scripture to combat the vulnerabilities inherent with old age as a defense in spiritual warfare.*

Throughout his ministry, Paul engages in spiritual warfare. Acts recounts the persecution he endures: soon after his conversion (Acts 9:22–25; 13:45–51; 14:2–6, 19; 16:19–26; 17:5–14; 18:12–17; 19:23–34); prophesied persecution in Jerusalem (Acts 21:11–14); then actual persecution (Acts

21:27–40); in this section Paul remains under arrest and appears in trials before Felix then Festus and king Agrippa; later he sails to Rome and lives under house arrest awaiting trial before Caesar (Acts 24:1—28:31). Essentially, Paul suffers persecution, imprisonment, and eventually execution for the latter part of his life after his conversion.[9] He continues ministry until his death in his mid-sixties.[10]

Based on what we know about Paul, he leads a very active life and, despite suffering from repeated beatings, stoning, and imprisonment, he displays uncommon vigor, courage, and faithfulness unabated to the very end. Indeed, his final words in 2 Tim 4:6–8 substantiate his finishing well:[11]

> For I am already being poured out as a drink offering, and the time of my departure has come. I have fought the good fight, I have finished the course, I have kept the faith; in the future there is reserved for me the crown of righteousness, which the Lord, the righteous Judge, will award to me on that day; and not only to me, but also to all who have loved his appearing.

Paul's life and hardship prompts a question for us: will we prove faithful and finish well? Our distance from Paul shortens because we belong to the same historical-redemptive period as he. *A hermeneutical principle states: the possibility of finding an edifying example increases when we modern readers can compare ourselves with a biblical character living within the same historical-redemptive period as us with whom we share critical spiritual characteristics, including advanced age.* We and Paul live between the First and Second Advents of Christ and after the Holy Spirit's arrival at Pentecost. Both of us belong to the body of Christ, call God our Father, and celebrate the sacrament of the new covenant, thereby "proclaim[ing] the Lord's death until he comes" (1 Cor 11:26). However, we quickly acknowledge an important

---

9. Eastman attempts to trace Paul's life and career based on information gleaned from Acts and the undisputed Pauline letters but also refers to the disputed letters with caution ("Paul: Outline of His Life," 34–56). Eastman follows modern critical scholarship in viewing Ephesians, Colossians, 2 Thessalonians, 1 and 2 Timothy, and Titus as not written by Paul. Eastman also examines the ancient extrabiblical source 1 Clement, likely a second century composition immediately following the apostolic period. Even though we evangelicals may differ from Eastman's assessment of the disputed letters, at least he factors them in but with skepticism.

10. Eastman, "Paul: Outline of His Life," 52. Eastman estimates Paul's career as spanning the period from his early thirties until his death at around his mid-sixties.

11. Eastman ("Paul: Outline of His Life," 36n7) cites Murphy-O'Connor who finds 2 Timothy authentic compared to the other two Pastoral epistles (*Paul: Critical Life*, 356–59).

difference—Paul is an apostle receiving direct divine revelation and composing a significant portion of the NT. Then we must discern what aspects of Paul's life and ministry we can strive to replicate and what other aspects remain unique to him. As discussed earlier, Scripture holds God's people, old and young, morally accountable. Then we can examine Paul's moral profile and use it as our benchmark. We can also pursue similar ministries as preaching, teaching, church planting, missions work, and mentoring. Likely we will face hardship and even persecution. We recognize, however, the historical and cultural differences between Paul and us. He ministers to Jews and gentiles, even though his primary calling focuses on gentiles. His Jewish kinsmen persecute him. A comparable scenario for us may be that we reach out to all, regardless of ethnicity or personal background and that our kinsmen may cause us difficulty, especially if they subscribe to different religious beliefs and practices. In multi-religious Asia where Christians represent a small minority, the chances that we encounter such challenges increase. But the supernatural aspects of Paul's ministry lie beyond our capability. Yet, we too should strive to prove faithful to the very end.

We began our discussion with spiritual warfare, something Paul engages in continually. In this conflict we too engage because Paul admonishes us to put on the full armor of God (Eph 6:10–17). We find encouragement in Paul's victories and escapes from certain demise by looking to our God for protection and guidance. Paul appeals to his readers to intercede on his behalf that he remains fearless as he makes known the mystery of the gospel (Eph 6:19–20). We have this mystery in our possession as well and for which we need boldness to proclaim. Finally, with Paul as our edifying example can we in turn edify others by our example?

Family Responsibility of the Aged

Specific consideration for the aged occurs in Scripture but only in a few incidences (for example, 1 Tim 5:1–16). The instructions in such cases are generally explicit. Although the original setting of the Timothy passage may be culturally conditioned, the context is based on church relationships rather than the family or other kind of group. But the fact that Paul uses familial terms, *father* and *mother*, in the passage above suggests that Paul regards the relationships between believers to approximate family dynamics. Regardless of the readers' cultural situation, whether collectivist or individualistic, instructions on the interactions between believers continue to be relevant today within the believing community. If no clear distinction is made between readers based on age, the text should be interpreted and applied without such distinction equally to all readers. Age, then, is not a hermeneutical factor generally unless Scripture makes a distinction.

However, Paul instructs Timothy to make a distinction between how he interacts with older members of his congregation and with those younger (1 Tim 5:1–2). Regard the older generation as fathers and mothers and the younger contingent as siblings, respectively. That perspective locates older believers within the purview of the command to honor one's parents (Exod 20:12; Deut 5:16) which Jesus reaffirms (Matt 15:4; 19:19; Mark 7:10; 10:19; Luke 18:20) and also Paul (Eph 6:2). Readers from Asian cultures can readily relate to Paul's familial allusions. Honor and shame characterize collectivistic societies. Paul ascribes honor to older people but the context suggests that this honor is also acquired. He instructs Timothy about proper conduct by all believers, male and female (1 Tim 2:8–15; 3:14–15; 4:1–11; 5:3–16; 6:1–2, 6–10, 17–19).[12] Proper conduct results in Paul's commendation and God's. Presuming this to be true for the older members of the church, they would not only be commended for behavior that befits all faithful believers but they receive additional recognition for being older. Then, it seems, that age as a highly valued characteristic brings about additional honor.[13]

In purposefully using familial terms, *father*, *mother*, *brother*, and *sister* (1 Tim 5:1–2), Paul depicts another important concept, kinship. Believers all belong to the same family with God as Father.[14] Living in a collectivist society, the first readers already value belonging to their respective groups, likely their biological family and possibly a guild if they are craftsmen, merchants, or soldiers. To declare a change in affiliation to a new group, the family of God, would imply new connections and the attendant responsibilities. The change may disrupt the old group where old ties may have to break in order to form new ties within the new group. This can result in broken relationships and hostile feelings, a very difficult situation. Then their identity changes as well. Heeding Paul's teaching, new believers have

---

12. Specific instructions to Timothy himself are not included in these verses cited but are found elsewhere.

13. Richards and James discuss the values that contribute to honor (*Misreading Scripture with Individualistic Eyes*, 134–36). As the authors note, a common goal across cultures and geographical regions is honor, but the values that contribute to acquiring that honor differ from culture to culture and people to people.

14. Richards and James, *Misreading Scripture with Individualistic Eyes*, 239–53.

a new set of parents and siblings that can be seen as a threat to biological parents and families. Then conversion is not only being born again and getting saved and justified on an individual level, but conversion also entails joining (Paul's term is *adoption*, Rom 8:15) a new community or family. Hence, *a hermeneutical principle emerges: regardless of personal background, whether individualistic or collectivistic, we automatically become spiritually collectivistic with the fundamental duty of loving and honoring one another within the believing community, and so read and interpret Scripture with this changed orientation*. We do not seek personal benefits only for ourselves but we also seek the benefit of others in our spiritual family. We ask how to interpret and apply God's word as a community of believers. Our allegiance is to God and his children and no longer to the world. As God's children, we have ascribed honor. He is the King and so we are royalty. But if we align well morally and spiritually with scriptural admonitions, having shared biblical values, we bring honor to our King and to our divine family. We also gain acquired honor having secured the Lord's approval.

Paul leaves the criteria for determining to which category (older or younger) a believer belongs, other than gender, open to Timothy's interpretation. But a few verses later (1 Tim 5:9), Paul distinguishes widows of at least 60 years of age and who have no supporting family as those deserving the church's support. The very next verse (1 Tim 5:10) lists the qualifications such a widow must satisfy before becoming eligible. She must have a proven track record of faithful service, caring for her family, and devotion to the Lord. These qualifications confirm the previous discussion, we older people ought to remain faithfully upright and pleasing to the Lord to the very end. A history of personal piety and loving service to the Lord and to others must continue into the present time and on into the future. Retirement from such faithfulness proves unscriptural.

Using Paul's age requirement as a threshold, we may conclude that believers over 60 years of age should be treated as fathers and mothers. However, this rule of thumb applies to Paul's time and not necessarily to our time. With the lengthening of life expectancy with improved medical technology and better understanding of healthy diets and life practices, we might not regard 60 as old. But attitudes toward what constitutes old age can vary from person to person and across cultures. Japan, for example, boasts the highest life expectancy in the world.[15] Perhaps the one important

---

15. Juneau, "Why Do the Japanese Have the Highest Life Expectancy?" The comparison is made among the G7 countries, where women enjoy significantly longer lives

opinion that really matters is our own. Do we consider someone as old? Due to one's relative health and vitality, how active a lifestyle is pursued, and whether one is still engaged in work, either as an employee, entrepreneur, or hobby, we decide where a person fits in.

But Paul places the responsibility on Timothy to decide who should be treated as a father or mother. So public perception is important. Within the church, do the leaders and fellow members see a person as old or, at least, as older? Proper respect and deference emerge. Especially in Asian culture, someone deemed older is often addressed as "uncle/auntie," communicating respect. *A hermeneutical principle states: if others within the believing community regard me as older, I can read and interpret Scripture as an older person in the role of a father or mother.*

This discussion serves as the background for presenting another hermeneutical principle, *the principle of imparting a legacy*. Our submission to scriptural mandates, faithfulness to the Lord, and care for others serve as a platform for influencing the younger generation, provided we have a proven, unbroken record of integrity and fruitfulness. Our interpretation of Scripture functions not only as a guide for ourselves but also as content and orientation for our instruction of younger believers. We are in a position to instruct, disciple, mentor, and advise. We read our Bibles in preparation for intentional interaction with others. What truths, principles, insights, and lessons can we extract from Scripture in order to instruct, exhort, and warn our younger contemporaries?

For us to be effective, we need to understand to some degree the language of the next generation. Even when speaking the same native tongue, there is the generational language gap where how one generation communicates differs in significant ways from another generation.[16] The challenge escalates if different generations speak different languages. This phenomenon appears in ethic churches. For example, my home church in America speaks three major languages (Mandarin, Cantonese, and English), where the older generation uses a Chinese dialect whereas the younger generation speaks English. Even within my own family, I cannot speak directly with

---

than the men who live only marginally longer than non-Japanese men. See also, Aetna, "Secrets of Japan's High Life Expectancy." A survey confirms sixty thousand centenarians in the country.

16. Welocalize, "Evolution of Language across Generations." Businesses, especially in marketing, recognize the co-existence of four generations (baby boomers, Generation X, millennials, Generation Z) to whom they wish to target their products. They realize the necessity of framing their message according to the native language of each generation.

my paternal grandmother, who speaks only her native tongue, which I do not know. In order to share the gospel with her, I employ an interpreter. Thankfully, the message got through and she professed faith in the Lord.

Two other factors come into consideration. First, we need to establish a functional relationship with the next generation. We take the initiative in showing care and interest in them. We invest time with them. Second, we must establish credibility.[17] Why should they listen to us and be open to our influence? Do they respect and trust us? We must earn that by our personal history of faithfulness to the Lord, mastery of Scripture, and genuine concern for them. Are we worthy role models for them to emulate?

Paul presents himself as an example for us to study and follow. In 1 Thess 2:7–8, 10–11, he writes:

> But we proved to be gentle among you. As a nursing mother tenderly cares for her own children, in the same way we had a fond affection for you and were delighted to share with you not only the gospel of God, but also our own lives, because you had become very dear to us. You are witnesses, and so is God, of how devoutly and rightly and blamelessly we behaved toward you believers; just as you know how we were exhorting and encouraging and imploring each one of you as a father would his own children.

When he first ministers to the Thessalonian Christians, he acts as a mother tenderly caring for her children and as a father exhorting, encouraging, and imploring his children. He behaves as a spiritual parent in birthing his readers by leading them to Christ and facilitating their initial journey in the faith. Even though we have not led someone to the faith, we can still serve as their spiritual mentor, discipler, teacher, or advisor. Hence, we read and study Scripture with the intent to pass on biblical truths. We formulate how to express these truths in understandable ways.

Scripture declares that Abraham is the father of Jews and gentiles who have his kind of faith (Rom 4:11–12). This relationship is categorically different than the one Paul has with his Thessalonian readers. Paul uses simile to compare himself with a mother or father in his loving ministry to them. He exhibits characteristics normally ascribed to parents. In contrast, Abraham is our father. The role of father for Abraham signifies him as the prototype of numerous descendants who are organically related to

---

17. Based on Aristotle's teachings, Kennedy introduces *ethos*, the character or credibility of a writer or speaker that ensures that the communication will be readily accepted (*New Testament Interpretation*, 15).

him spiritually.[18] In that sense, Abraham is our progenitor and, hence, we resemble our father in his faith.[19] We are in Abraham's family with him as father and we as his children. As a direct consequence, we inherit the promise given to Abraham (Gal 3:9, 14), as Paul proclaims (Rom 8:16–17), "The Spirit himself testifies with our spirit that we are children of God, and if children, heirs also, heirs of God and fellow heirs with Christ, if indeed we suffer with him so that we may also be glorified with him." The substance of our inheritance consists of two elements: justification by faith and the gift of the Holy Spirit (Gal 3:14).[20]

We older people can strive to imitate Paul and Abraham for their lifelong faithfulness to the Lord. We can also emulate their faith. But Paul and Abraham are unique: the former is an apostle, and God makes a covenant with and through the latter to bless all of us, regardless of personal background and, as a result, we become children of God (Gal 3:26–28), Abraham's seed and heirs to the promise (Gal 3:29). As older believers we read Gal 3:28 ("There is neither Jew nor Greek, there is neither slave nor free, there is neither male nor female; for you are all one in Christ Jesus") to encompass the added truth: "there is no distinction between the old and young." This declassification applies to membership in the family of God; we are all equally included in that family. But, as Paul admonishes in 1 Tim 5:1–2, the church should exercise deferential treatment toward the older generation. Can we graciously receive such deference with dignity? At the same time, can we leverage that position to minister to those younger? Age potentially offers us the credibility we need to influence. Thus, our practice of *the hermeneutical principle of imparting a legacy* can unify the body of Christ as the older and younger members draw closer together.

---

18. Tan, "Rhetoric of Abraham's Faith," 211. Tan labels Abraham a superordinate prototype. Commentators regard Abraham as an example of faith. For example, Fitzmyer writes of Abraham's spiritual paternity and example (*Romans*, 381–82) and his faith as the type for all who are credited as righteous as he (*Romans*, 388). According to Matera, Abraham is our model of faith (*Romans*, 119). But Abraham is more than simply our example or model, otherwise he is no different than Paul in that regard.

19. Tan describes Abraham's relationship with his descendants as a patrilineal descent ("Rhetoric of Abraham's Faith," 212).

20. Fung, *Galatians*, 151–52.

Learning from Aged Biblical Characters

Biblical characters depicted as aged raise some questions for the reader. One, is age an important narrative aspect in the portrayal that affects the telling of the story or is it only incidental? Two, if age assumes an important role in the narrative, does it have moral or spiritual implications for the character and the unfolding story? Three, what important insights might aged readers extract from the character? Are these insights affirming the value of the aged in society or in God's program? Or do these insights present a cautionary note for the aged? A classic example is King Solomon, who begins his reign exceptionally well and prospers beyond measure. However, the narrative goes on to state (1 Kgs 11:1–4):

> Now King Solomon loved many foreign women along with the daughter of Pharaoh: Moabite, Ammonite, Edomite, Sidonian, and Hittite women, from the nations of which the Lord had said to the sons of Israel, "You shall not associate with them, nor shall they associate with you; they will certainly turn your heart away to follow their gods." Solomon clung to these in love. He had seven hundred wives, who were princesses, and three hundred concubines; and his wives turned his heart away. For when Solomon was old, his wives turned his heart away to follow other gods; and his heart was not wholly devoted to the Lord his God, as the heart of his father David had been.

Two significant observations merit highlighting. First, Solomon already violates God's prohibition about loving foreign women who would lead him into idolatry relatively early in his rule and life. Second, when he enters old age, his resistance to their temptation apparently lessens to the point where he succumbs to idolatry. The point at which he falls cannot be located precisely except, perhaps, when he first enters compromising relationships. The sheer number of such relationships correlates with his extravagance as he pursues every luxury without restriction. The narrative suggests that Solomon's downward spiral exacerbates when he is old. But the text does not offer precision—how old is he when he becomes old? 60 or older? A little younger, maybe in his fifties? We don't know. But perhaps the important point is that, for Solomon, becoming old signifies his abandoning his famed wisdom so that he acts foolishly, without moral or spiritual restraint. "His heart was not wholly devoted to the Lord his God, as the heart of his father David had been."

Unfortunately, our questions cannot be answered as the narrative simply tells the story without much explanation. It is less a character study and more a depiction of why Israel split into two kingdoms, north and south. Solomon's unfaithfulness incurs God's displeasure and, as a consequence, a sizable portion of his domain is given to another (1 Kgs 11:11), but his son would retain the throne because of God's faithfulness to his covenant promise to David (1 Kgs 11:13). Hence, as readers we must recognize that Solomon becoming old is only a relatively minor point in the narrative. Although he still serves as a caution to us older readers, we should not ignore the bigger picture drawn.

The bigger picture will certainly prevent us from drawing a totally unwarranted application—you can enjoy the perks of being a sugar daddy as a rich old man. More germane to the overall story is that God's judgment of Solomon and the catastrophic consequences to the nation portray the seriousness of God's demand for total allegiance. Solomon's advanced age does not lessen the consequences, that is, God does not lessen his expectations and demands on an old man nor soften his dealing with him. Age does not excuse one to become delinquent to one's moral and spiritual responsibilities. We may conclude, therefore, that biblical commands about morality, spirituality, and reverence toward God apply to everyone, regardless of age, gender, or other social status. *Even with a distinct hermeneutics of ageism, the interpretation of one's moral and spiritual responsibility to the Lord does not differentiate between the young and old. Hence, there would be no recourse for a hermeneutics of suspicion that characterizes feminist and ecological readings, as Scripture does not evidence a bias against the aged.* As a positive spin, we may note that God does not discriminate his call for personal holiness and devotion to him based solely on age. We older folks cannot excuse ourselves from accountability to our Lord because of a diminished moral or spiritual capacity. That capacity remains fully functional even when our physical strength and stamina are waning. But if someone suffers mental deterioration gravitating toward dementia,[21] will God still hold them accountable to the same degree as before? Scripture does not provide a clear statement on that. However, we note a pattern of accommodation, where God factors in the person's ability or condition—for example,

---

21. The American Psychological Association defines dementia as "memory impairment, cognitive disturbances and disturbances in executive functioning (i.e., goal setting) that result in significant impairment in social or occupational functioning and represent a significant decline from a previous level of functioning" (*ScienceDirect* editors, "Senility").

Moses's hesitancy, perhaps due to fear, to represent God before pharaoh and the Israelites in Egypt, Gideon and his fleece to acquire added assurance of victory, young Samuel before he recognizes God's voice, and feeding an exhausted Elijah after the Mount Carmel confrontation. So we may hope for similar accommodation for those suffering the ravages of old age.

As affirmation that age does not handicap us, we recall a couple of examples of men approaching the end of life who still exert a powerful spiritual influence. First, we read about Jacob blessing his grandsons, Joseph's children (Gen 48:9–20), and prophesying the future of each of his sons as he blesses them (Gen 49:1–28). Significantly, the narrative states (Gen 49:28): "All these are the twelve tribes of Israel, and this is what their father said to them when he blessed them. He blessed them, every one with the blessing appropriate to him." In spite of his advanced age, being 147 at the time (Gen 47:28), Jacob retains his mental and spiritual faculties, apparently without discernable degradation. He understands the character of each of his sons accurately. The fact that the observation about Jacob comes from the narrator's point of view reassures us of its accuracy. Indeed, we may presume that his point of view reflects the divine point of view. In this incidence, Jacob functions as a prophet.

Second, when Joshua summons all of Israel's leaders, he "was old, advanced in years" (Josh 23:1). He issues a strong challenge to them (Josh 23:6–8): "Be very determined, then, to keep and do everything that is written in the Book of the Law of Moses, so that you will not turn aside from it to the right or to the left, so that you will not associate with these nations, these which remain with you, or mention the name of their gods, or make anyone swear by them, or serve them, or bow down to them. But you are to cling to the Lord your God, as you have done to this day." Joshua then renews the covenant with the people to serve the Lord and to abstain from acknowledging foreign gods (Josh 24:1–28). They reconfirm allegiance to the Lord. In challenging them to decide on whom to serve, Joshua boldly declares, "As for me and my house, we will serve the Lord" (Josh 24:15f). He presents himself as an influential example to emulate. We may also affirm that he functions as the spiritual leader in his family.

Before we dismiss Jacob and Joshua as being unique, a one-of-a-kind character each greatly used by God to advance his purposes for his chosen people, impossible to follow as examples, we should note one aspect of each man's character and action that lies within our reach. Both care deeply for their children and for their people. They continue to exert a powerful moral and spiritual influence. In fact, we surmise that their advanced age and lifelong consistency grant them positions of honor and respect. Their words carry weight. And they exercise timely actions that bless many others. We might even say that this is an important part of their legacy.

These two examples prompt *a hermeneutical question: how do we discern what is unique, not to be emulated, and what can serve as a model for today?* Certainly, both men serve a very strategic role in furthering Israel's history as God's people in claiming God's covenantal promises. In that sense, they are unique in fulfilling their narrative roles. At the same time, however, they are human with family and responsibilities to others. But we may hesitate identifying with them in their old age, rationalizing that perhaps God enables them to pursue a lengthy career to the very end, neither retiring per se. Jacob demonstrates prophetic insight about his sons, each of whom will produce entire tribes, and Joshua still commands an entire nation in the end. They are like Moses where the narrative states (Deut 34:7): "Although Moses was 120 years old when he died, his eyesight was not dim, nor had his vigor left him." But the narrative informs us explicitly that Jacob suffers age-related weakness (Gen 48:1–2). And Joshua may have hinted that his military career is expiring because of age (Josh 23:2). Moses, then, is the exception.

Let me suggest *a principle of scalability*. Both Jacob and Joshua personify the top of the scale; the scope of their influence encompasses a vast domain comprising many people beyond their immediate families. Their location on the scale reflects their narrative importance. We, on the other hand, have importance too, relatively speaking. But we find ourselves further down the scale where the domain of our influence covers a footprint significantly smaller. We share some practices with our illustrious spiritual ancestors (Rom 4:16–17). We know our children as does Jacob and desire to bless them. We urge our kinsmen in the faith to stay faithful to the Lord as we strive to exercise spiritual oversight of our families. A significant aspect of our legacy is our witness as someone who remains faithful to the end of our journey. We model for our family and for the believing community. We model for our neighbors in the greater community. We care, showing compassion with the opportunity. We can offer encouragement and advice when approached.

Scalability means we do not attempt to imitate what the biblical character does to the same degree of difficulty or magnitude. We are not prophetic like Jacob, although we can be anticipatory and hopeful about our children. We do not summon an entire nation like Joshua and present our family as a model. We can strive to be exemplary before our neighbors even if they constitute only our next-door neighbors. We extract the principle and then apply it based on our ability and opportunity. Thus, we may express *the hermeneutical principle of scalability in two parts: first, separate out a biblical character's abilities and narrative role that can exceed our own talents and differ from our stewardship as not something to emulate, except on a more limited scale; and second, strive to emulate the admirable virtues that characterize them as what God expects from us*. We discern the biblical character's traits and qualities to pursue for ourselves. Such virtues are not scalable but should describe us fully. For example, Joseph's faithfulness to the Lord throughout his life should characterize us. Then we estimate the extent to which we can follow their deeds and accomplishments and scale them down to within our reach. In this regard, we can check ourselves periodically over the years to affirm our consistency. Are we as fervent for the Lord and his enterprise as before when we were younger? Recalling Solomon's career but filtering out his opulence and unrivaled wisdom, do we discern any downward spiral of decreasing vigilance over our conduct or increasing false sense of security that we would not fall after years of maintaining our integrity?

Narrative and Theological Roles of the Age Progression of Biblical Characters

Biblical narratives that track characters through relatively long periods in life afford the reader the opportunity to trace the possible effects of aging over time. We find, for example, Jacob as a newborn with his twin brother Esau (Gen 25:22–26). The Lord's prophecy about two nations in Rebekah's womb where the older will serve the younger immediately sets Jacob and Esau apart from the rest of humanity, including us readers. The narrative then passes over the boys' youth before commenting about them in adulthood where Esau is described as a skilled hunter and Jacob as a homebody (Gen 25:27). Twice Jacob takes advantage of Esau in taking his birthright when he is famished (Gen 25:29–34) and, through the advice and coaxing of his mother, he deceives Isaac to cheat Esau out of his blessing (Gen 27:1–41). At the time both are over 40 years old (Esau's age when he married two Hittite women to the grief of his parents, Gen 26:34–35; but we don't know how many years later that Isaac's deception takes place). In order to escape Esau's subsequent wrath, Jacob flees to Paddan-Aram, his mother's birthplace. The journey from Beersheba to Paddan-Aram is roughly 450 miles. Traveling on foot indicates Jacob's good health and stamina. He sojourns in Paddan-Aram twenty years (Gen 31:38) before returning to his parents. During a night of his return journey, Jacob wrestles with a man, possibly the angel of the Lord, all night until dawn and prevails to gain the blessing (Gen 32:24–30). At this point, Jacob will likely be over 60 years old, remarkably strong enough to wrestle for such a long time.

Through his forties, fifties, and into his sixties to some extent, Jacob exhibits the vigor to shepherd Laban's flocks and his own (Gen 29:20–30; 30:35–43). Measuring a character's age when the narrative does not give regular and precise updates becomes a guesstimate. Tending sheep and goats demands enduring the heat of the day and cold of night, with plenty of fresh air. Leading a relatively sedentary life, we cannot identify with Jacob nor compare to his physical stamina and health.

Later, Jacob's sons shepherd his flocks while he stays at home. We cannot conclude with certainty that he is too old and must have his sons replace him. Rather, his sons are old enough to assume responsibility and he may have passed the care of the flock to them. During this period, Joseph enters the narrative as a central figure at 17 years of age (Gen 37:2). After a number of events involving him—sold by his brothers as a slave (Gen 37:25–28); initially a servant of Potiphar, captain of pharaoh's guard (Gen 37:36; 39:1–6ab); falsely accused by Potiphar's wife and subsequently imprisoned (Gen 39:7–23); interprets the dreams of two fellow prisoners that are fulfilled (Gen 40:1–23); two full years later pharaoh has dreams that Joseph interprets that enable Egypt to prepare for a future famine lasting seven years after seven years of abundance (Gen 41:1–36); appointed second to pharaoh to oversee the storage of grain (Gen 41:37–45); being 30 years old when entering pharaoh's service (Gen 41:46); the famine unfolds prompting everyone in Egypt and elsewhere to purchase grain from Joseph (Gen 41:53–57); the episodes of Joseph's brothers coming to buy grain (Gen 42:1—45:15); pharaoh invites Jacob to come to Egypt (Gen 45:17–20)—Joseph finally meets Jacob for an emotional reunion (Gen 46:29–30) and introduces him to pharaoh (Gen 47:7), who asks his age, whereupon Jacob answers, 130 years old (Gen 47:8–10). On the journey to Egypt at pharaoh's invitation, Jacob rides a cart (Gen 45:27), as do his daughters-in-law and grandchildren (Gen 46:5). The necessity of the cart suggests that Jacob is too old to travel any other way. In his final illness, Jacob receives the visit of Joseph with his two sons (Gen 48:1–22). Informed of the visitors, Jacob must strengthen himself to sit up in bed (Gen 48:2).[22] His failing eyesight represents another indication of his advanced age (Gen 48:10).

In his final seventeen years, from his traveling to Egypt to being bedridden, Jacob loses all mobility and strength. When introduced to pharaoh, Jacob can walk and presumably stand before the king (Gen 47:7–10). Yet, even on his deathbed, Jacob can still deliver a rather lengthy blessing to all his sons (Gen 49:1–28) and give some final instructions (Gen 49:29–33). His mind remains sharp.

Hermeneutically, we look for any clues about a character's age and age-related characteristics. The information may serve as a time-element in giving the reader the sense of the passage of time. In Jacob's and Joseph's cases, the successive ages provided reveal a significant passage of time where jumps in the narrative signal the omission of biographical data as the narrative fast-forwards between recorded events. We ask about the implications of the mention of any age in the narrative. For example, we commiserate with Joseph's enslavement at such a young age and his father's anguish at his assumed demise. And we wonder at Jacob's physical stamina in the all-night wrestling match when he is likely in his sixties. The narrative informs us that both men assume important roles in the unfolding of the divine plan. God reappears to Jacob at Bethel promising him a community of nations, kings among his descendants, and the land first promised to Abraham and Isaac (Gen 35:1–15), after an earlier dream on his way to Paddan-Aram (Gen 28:10–22). Essentially, God reaffirms the promise to Abraham, now repeated to Jacob, of the land, many descendants, and being the channel of blessing to all peoples of the earth. Additionally, God reassures Jacob of his eventual return back to the land of promise, whereupon Jacob states his contingent acknowledgment of the Lord as his God should the Lord bring him back safely. Given the length of his sojourn in the land of his mother's birth, we calculate the time between the two divine visitations. Although two decades will pass, Jacob does not accuse God of unfaithfulness or delay in fulfilling his word. Laban cheats Jacob ten times by changing his wages but he experiences the Lord's continued protection (Gen 31:7). As readers, we may easily ignore the passage of significant amounts of time, as the narrated events are not covered in real-time. However, if we place ourselves

---

22. Hamilton notes that Jacob is bedridden and "had to exert himself: he *rallied his strength (wayyithazzēq)*, for it took great effort for him even to sit up" (*Genesis, Chapters 18–50*, 628).

in Jacob's place and wonder whether we might not begin to doubt God's promises as we face yet another reversal of fortune, we understand Jacob's conditional trust in the Lord as we look to an uncertain future.

All the while, Jacob ages and, no doubt, he realizes that his parents are also aging. Should he return, will he see them alive? At 40, Isaac marries Rebekah (Gen 25:20). But we do not know his age when his twin sons are born. But because Rebekah is childless, requiring Isaac's intercessory prayer on her behalf (Gen 25:21), some time must have passed before the birth. On his return trip, Jacob being over 60 implies that Isaac would be over 100 years old. With a life span of 180 years (Gen 35:28), he would spend quite a few years with Jacob on his return.

As interesting as tracking the ages of characters in the biblical narrative may be, the reason for Scripture even mentioning the numbers is to provide us readers a benchmark to assess God's faithfulness, the covenant promises he makes and fulfills especially to Abraham, Isaac, and Jacob. The Lord utilizes both the natural processes (taking years to complete in the ordinary events of life) and supernatural interventions in overcoming obstacles that lie outside the realm of human endeavor in order to fulfill his word. In twenty years, Jacob transitions from being single to being the father of many sons (Gen 35:22–26). Through interpreting divinely inspired dreams that forecast the future and wise administration of a nation's food production and storage, Joseph saves Egypt and his extended family from severe famine. Indeed, from the perspective of over twenty years of hardship and separation from his family (enslaved to Ishmaelites traveling to Egypt at 17 to being 30 when he begins serving pharaoh, through seven years of plenty and two years into the famine, Gen 45:6), Joseph declares to his brothers (Gen 50:19b–21a): "Do not be afraid, for am I in God's place? As for you, you meant evil against me, but God meant it for good in order to bring about this present result, to keep many people alive. So therefore, do not be afraid; I will provide for you and your little ones."

From our perspective the extraordinary life spans of some biblical characters (Abraham, Isaac, Jacob, and Joseph) who live beyond 100 years seem a bit farfetched, as modern life expectancy usually tops off in the eighties, although we know of exceptions. The process of aging seems much more protracted for them as compared to us. But as discussed in the previous couple of paragraphs, the recorded aging provides the benchmark for assessing how God fulfills his promises as circumstances unfold. He does not do things instantaneously but utilizes the natural processes that mark individual lives and that of nations. Simultaneously, we readers may examine the faith and faithfulness of these characters over the years, often decades. Even when their physical vitality declines, their spiritual and moral vigor remains steadfast. God still uses them as servants and as a blessing to others. *Regarding the characters' mentioned ages as a theological benchmark, we offer a hermeneutical principle: characters' ages and progressive aging serve as a narrative time marker to give readers the sense of God's faithfulness to his promises and of the gradual unfolding of his plans over the years.* The selective telling of the story ensures that readers do not get bogged down by minutiae so that they can stay focused on the big picture depicting God as the main actor. Readers, then, can more readily sense the divine movement with the narrative's fast-forwarding by-passing appreciable lengths of time. There is almost a panoramic sweep that takes our breath away, leaving us more amazed at God's sovereign rule in and over history. Given their extensive life spans, the characters, namely the patriarchs and Joseph, enjoy front-row seats to witness events unfold and gain a perspective of God in action, as Joseph states in Gen 50:20 after surveying his career. We readers can vicariously experience and witness events from the characters' perspective and thereby gain deeper understanding of the divine story.

At the human level of the narrative, we see that God does not lessen his expectations and demands on his servants as they grow old. The apostle Paul exemplifies lifelong stewardship when he writes (2 Tim 4:6–8): "For I am already being poured out as a drink offering, and the time of my departure has come. I have fought the good fight, I have finished the course, I have kept the faith; in the future there is reserved for me the crown of righteousness, which the Lord, the righteous Judge, will award to me on that day; and not only to me, but also to all who have loved his appearing." May we prove as faithful when we enter and live out our later years.

Alternative Benchmark of the Age Progression of Biblical Characters

An alternative measure of a character's age comes from the mention of a monarch and the year of his reign. In Daniel, the titular character is time stamped to particular kings as the narrative unfolds. In chapter 1, Daniel and his three friends are chosen from among the youths to be exiled and trained for the king's service. This first deportation occurs in Nebuchadnezzar's first year (605 BCE).[23] Later in his second year, he has a dream which only Daniel can identify and interpret (Dan 2:1–45). Some time later, Nebuchadnezzar has another dream requiring Daniel's interpretation—a great tree dominates the landscape (Dan 4:1–27). Divine judgment calls for cutting down the tree leaving only the stump. The decree targets the king who will live among the wild animals for "seven times" (Dan 4:25).[24] Twelve months later, the king suffers the judgment's verdict (Dan 4:28–34).

In Daniel 5, Belshazzar is now king.[25] His father, Nebuchadnezzar, died in 562 BCE. But his own reign proves short-lived upon his assassination later that evening after the feast (Dan 5:30). His death occurs in 560 BCE.[26] Then Darius the Mede assumes rule (Dan 5:31).[27] At this point in history, Daniel has lived in Babylon for about forty-five years, assuming his deportation in 605 BCE. If we suggest that he is a young man of 17 when he arrives, then he would be approximately 62 years of age. Some time later, jealousy among his fellow administrators instigates the issuing of an edict that he violates because of his devotion to the Lord, whereupon they throw him into the lion's den (Dan 6:1–16). The verb *to throw* or *cast* also appears in the episode of the king's soldiers casting Daniel's three friends into the fiery furnace (Dan 3:20–21, 24). The action depicts rough treatment. Whereas the friends are relatively young at the time, Daniel is advanced in age. Somehow, he survives the rough handling. Later, his accusers and their families get thrown into the den (Dan 6:24). As a concluding statement to the episode, the narrative states (Dan 6:28): "So this Daniel enjoyed success in the reign of Darius, and in the reign of Cyrus the Persian." A marginal reading of the verse in the NIV has "Darius, that is, in the reign of Cyrus the Persian." This rendering supports identifying Darius and Cyrus as the same individual. Historically, Media and Persia formed a united kingdom as depicted in Daniel's vision (Dan 8:3–4, 20). Cyrus the Great defeats the

---

23. Pritchard, *Ancient Near East*, 205.

24. Rather than speculating, it may behoove us to leave the expression "seven times" uninterpreted. See, for example, Widder ("Letting Nebuchadnezzar Speak," 209). However, Oshima posits seven years ("Nebuchadnezzar's Madness," 667). Oshima views Daniel 4 as a literary motif taken from cuneiform literature, particularly Sumero-Akkadian prayers and lamentations.

25. In 2 Kgs 25:27, he is called Awel-Marduk.

26. According to the Uruk King List, he is identified as Amîl-Marduk.

27. Darius is not mentioned in extrabiblical sources prompting debate among scholars as to his historicity. See Finley, "Who Wrote the Book of Daniel? Part 2." Finley proposes that Darius the Mede and Cyrus the Persian are the same person.

Median Empire in 539 BCE and establishes the Persian Empire (or Achaemenid Empire). According to Dan 1:21, Daniel continues until the first year of Cyrus or 539 BCE. That implies that Daniel lives until the age of about 83. The biblical account states that he prospers throughout that period. However, Dan 10:1 records Daniel receiving a revelation in Cyrus's third year, pushing Daniel's age to about 85.[28]

The significant point we derive is that God continues to actively engage Daniel as a prophet and likely as an administrator with important responsibilities. No hint of slowing down or of a reduced workload emerges. Daniel is fully functional in pursuing his duties. Clearly, his mental and spiritual faculties continue unabated. Physically, he may not be as spry as in years past. But he still exhibits vigor. We detect no hint that he ever retires. Over all these years he exerts a powerful influence over rulers and others.

Before we credit Daniel's unusual physical fitness in his later years, we should consider another factor to explain why God continues to use him. Two incidences in his life offer insight into his character. First, as a youth, Daniel resolves not to defile himself with the royal food and so God honors his resolve by giving him and his friends wisdom and learning far superior to that of all the other youths undergoing the same training (Dan 1:8–20). Daniel also understands visions and dreams. Second, he proves an exceptional administrator not only in skill but also in trustworthiness, honesty, and diligence (Dan 6:3–4). Moreover, he refuses to direct his prayers to the king despite the royal edict threatening certain death for noncompliance in order to remain faithful to his God (Dan 6:6–13). These two episodes span nearly all of Daniel's life and service. His defining characteristic is faithfulness to the Lord and offering his best in whatever he pursues.

Age, then, fades as a critical factor. Rather, faithfulness to God by maintaining one's purity and integrity and serving with all diligence move to the forefront. If this important principle describes us, will our Lord not continue to use us regardless of our age? Even if we cannot perform some things we used to do earlier in life, we can still serve him in some capacity.

---

28. For the apparent contradiction between Dan 1:21 and Dan 10:1, see Seow (*Daniel*, 153). Seow sees no contradiction. In 1:21, the adverb "there," i.e., where Daniel remains until Cyrus's first year, refers to merely a geographical location, not to the city of Babylon per se, as the Babylonian Empire ceases existence with the ascension of Cyrus. Consequently, Seow dates Cyrus's third year at 536 BCE. Di Lella clarifies the matter by noting that Daniel continues in the Babylonian court until Cyrus's first year, implying that Daniel's service to the Babylonians ends but not that he dies (*Daniel, Chapters 1–9*, 277).

As we mentioned in a previous section, the narrative thrust is not Daniel, although he remains the most prominent human character, except when his three friends are cast into the hot furnace (Dan 3:1–30), and when Nebuchadnezzar recalls his dream to Daniel forecasting his humiliation for pride (Dan 4:1–18) and the dream's fulfillment twelve months later (Dan 4:28–37), and when Belshazzar sees the writing on the wall (Dan 5:1–9). But even in the latter two incidences, Daniel emerges as the heroic interpreter of the dream and the writing. In these three episodes, the main actor is God who protects Daniel's friends and pronounces judgment on the two kings. In each case, God shows himself superior to human kings, regardless of their power and authority. In his own narration of the visions about beasts and their interpretation, Daniel clearly credits God as the source who knows the future and fate of nations. At the conclusion of recounting these visions, an angelic messenger pronounces the eventual destruction of these powerful nations as the precursor to establishing God's eternal kingdom (Dan 7:26–27; 8:25c foresees the victory achieved by the Prince of princes). Then Daniel receives another revelation about the future involving political intrigue and military exploits by various rulers and end time events including the resurrection of the dead (Dan 10:1—12:13).

This overview of the book of Daniel provides us with the reason why Daniel lives and serves for so long, from youth to old age. He is God's chosen instrument to reveal the divine message in the form of dreams and visions given progressively over the decades while in exile. He occupies a strategic role as prophet, delivering some messages to kings, demonstrating to them that there is a God above who judges powerful kings; but other messages appear as private communique for him to record for posterity (Dan 12:4). His age, although advanced toward the end of his career, recedes from prominence. It is not a prominent factor. We cannot, then, simply draw lessons about old age from his story. Hence, *a hermeneutical principle states that the narrative and its emphasis are the determinative factors for discerning whether a character's age plays an important role in the story or not. A corollary principle suggests that, even if a character's age does not play an explicit role in the narrative, it may still offer valuable insights on a person's character trait so long as readers do not subvert the narrative's major points.*

God sovereignly chooses Daniel to prophesy. We might then argue that Daniel is the "perfect" choice given his faithfulness and exemplary character. But his three friends appear to be equally qualified. So why Daniel? As the dreams and visions occur, Daniel serves only as the interpreter totally reliant on God for the import. He is more an accessory standing at the margins as God takes center stage to proclaim his sovereign authority over all the nations, rebuking kings that fail to acknowledge him, and his plans that span much of history. At the end of history God's kingdom stands triumphant and continues into eternity.

We infer that Daniel understands his place and does not make Nebuchadnezzar's mistake of arrogantly boasting (Dan 4:30). Daniel depends on God for all interpretations of dreams and riddles and gives God the credit (Dan 2:18–23, 27–28). And God continues to use him for as long as visions are forthcoming, historically up to Cyrus's third year (Dan 10:1). Significantly, after recording that last vision, the narrative ends. Whether Daniel lives any longer remains a moot point and so we infer that the question is not critical. Then we ask, Would not a servant continue serving for as long as God continues to use them like in Daniel's case? Such a pattern motivates us to discern and accept opportunities even in old age. There is no retirement from serving our Lord.

We should avoid the mistake of moralizing from the text while ignoring the bigger picture. But, in recalling the gallery of the heroes of the faith in Hebrews 11, we find brief summaries of how some of them demonstrate faith (Heb 11:4–31) and a collective commentary about the rest (Heb 11:32–38). Mentioning all these characters appears to take them out of context in focusing on the motif of faith. Is not Scripture itself moralizing? Can we not do the same? After all, Scripture is a moral document revealing God's moral nature and demands on his moral creatures. Thus, we can extract moral principles from the text so long as we observe the corollary principle stated above. Curiously, we notice that Daniel is not explicitly named in Hebrews 11. However, a clear reference to him appears in Heb 11:33d ("who by faith . . . shut the mouths of lions"). This one allusion to Daniel ignores all the other episodes recorded in the book of Daniel. True. But the writer of Hebrews needs only one example that typifies Daniel's faith to make his point. So long as that one illustration shows Daniel's true character and is not the exception where he demonstrates faith just one time, then the writer's point remains valid. So if we've made the effort to comprehend the bigger picture within which a particular text resides then, I believe, we can extract a moral lesson from that text and situate it within the bigger picture.

The Urgency and Steadfastness of the Aged

Given the observation that the moral commandments, decrees, and exhortations in the Bible are directed to all God's people without explicit regard for age, then, for the most part, no special accommodation needs to be made hermeneutically. Since the Lord does not lighten the moral or ethical demands for us older folks, we cannot afford to slack off. We remain ever vigilant. Attention to the parables (ten virgins and bags of gold) urging listeners to continued alertness in order to remain faithful until the Lord returns speaks to us powerfully. The Olivet Discourse (particularly Matt 24:36—25:30; Mark 13:32–37; and Luke 21:34–36) exhorts us to watch (Mark 13:37; Luke 21:36). Paul reinforces this admonition (1 Thess 5:1–11). His desire to be with the Lord after dispensing with his earthly tent may resonate with us struggling with our aged bodies (2 Cor 5:1–5). Thus, we ought to share his ambition (2 Cor 5:9–10): "Therefore we also have as our ambition, whether at home or absent, to be pleasing to him. For we must all appear before the judgment seat of Christ, so that each one may receive compensation for his deeds done through the body, in accordance with what he has done, whether good or bad." As we draw closer to our end of this life, we become more acutely aware of the judgment seat of Christ. The sense of final accountability increases. We share Paul's "fear of the Lord" (2 Cor 5:11), prompting us to live and serve the Lord more intentionally, knowing that opportunities will soon end.

Then *the hermeneutical principle that should grip us with great sobriety is the principle of the urgent.* There has been much discussion about contrasting the urgent versus the important. A convenient graphic is the "Urgent versus Important Matrix."[29] Four quadrants depict the four possible scenarios: urgent but not important, urgent and important, not urgent or important, and not urgent but important. Scripture's moral and spiritual standards and decrees are important, non-negotiables. But for the aged, conforming to Scripture takes on added urgency. Of course, no one at any age can afford to think they can ignore God's word and have time to repent later. But older people are all too aware of the approaching end and inevitable accountability. This realization compels us to take our responsibility to the Lord more seriously than, perhaps, when we were younger, thinking that we have so much of life left and being preoccupied with our pursuits. Hence, we read Scripture with greater urgency than before. As the Bible

---

29. Elsey, "Urgent Important Matrix."

warns us, no one knows when their time of accountability will occur, so it is best that we remain ever watchful as faithful stewards (Matt 25:1–30).

We recall God's words to Ezekiel as the watchman (Ezek 33:1–16) to warn his people of God's justice (Ezek 33:12–13):

> And you, son of man, say to your fellow citizens, "The righteousness of a righteous one will not save him on the day of his offense, and as for the wickedness of a wicked one, he will not stumble because of it on the day when he turns from his wickedness; whereas a righteous one will not be able to live by his righteousness on the day when he commits sin." When I say to the righteous that he will certainly live, and he so trusts in his righteousness that he commits injustice, none of his righteous deeds will be remembered; but for that same injustice of his which he has committed he will die.

We may look back over a long life of righteousness before the Lord and find satisfaction. However, the day we smugly trust in our past and commit sin, the Lord will hold us guilty and our exemplary record will not save us from the consequences. We must remain faithfully upright and pleasing to the Lord to the very end. This perspective of God's justice, then, brings out another *hermeneutical principle: interpreting all moral and ethical demands as continually relevant throughout all of life to the very end*. Past obedience will not cover present disobedience, nor will present righteousness excuse future unrighteousness. Old age does not exempt us; we must remain faithful all the way until the Lord calls us home. A lifetime of fidelity and integrity is wasted if we fail morally at the end. It may seem harsh but Scripture is clear on the matter. Thus, we should read it earnestly and submit to its authority lest we become overly confident and even smug, thinking that after a long life of faith we can simply coast to the finish line.

For us older readers, the two closely related hermeneutical principles highlight our particular challenge as we read Scripture submissively. The principle of the urgent magnifies the importance of the present moment, the "now," not later even if it is later today. None of us knows the time of our end when the Lord calls us home. Paul is prepared to meet the Lord, even prefers that, but fruitful ministry to his readers prompts him to desire more time in this life (Phil 1:20–26). We can adopt Paul's mindset—ever ready to appear before the Lord should the time be now but also ever burdened to continue a little longer in this world should opportunities to minister and to bless others present themselves.

In Psalm 90, Moses meditates on the brevity of human life.[30] The motif of God's wrath toward human moral failure dominates this psalm. The sharp contrast between God and humans, his eternality versus their transience, his righteous indignation against their sinfulness, creates a strong sense of distance and dread. From God's perspective a thousand years seem like a single day (Ps 90:4), but from the human point of view seventy years or even eighty represent a whole lifetime, yet marked by trouble and sorrow (Ps 90:10). We affirm that life is tough. Now in my mid-seventies, whenever I survey my past, I wonder at how fleeting the years have been. What have I accomplished? Memories of struggle and failure linger more vividly than successes. Now my mortality stares at me in the face. The repeated references to God's wrath (Ps 90:7–11) move us to be mindful of our accountability to him and cause us to fear him (Ps 90:7, 11). Then comes the petition (Ps 90:12): "So teach us to number our days, that we may present to you a heart of wisdom." The wise recognize the brevity of life and the inescapability of God's wrath and, hence, strive to submit to him.[31] We need to maximize the opportunities to serve the Lord as we number our days, making each day count. Thus, *the hermeneutical principles of the urgent and of the continual relevance of our moral and ethical responsibilities throughout our lives to the very end represent our stewardship as we read and meditate on Scripture*. With these principles in mind, we ask, "What does the word demand of me now? And what must I observe and obey through the rest of my life?" We will be wise as we beseech the Lord to "confirm the work of our hands" (Ps 90:17).

A Closer Look at Abraham

What precautions do we take when we examine a biblical character as a potential model or example for us to imitate? We have already mentioned Abraham earlier as a model of faith. As noted earlier, Abraham's amazing life span of 175 years places him way beyond any practical consideration

---

30. Whereas the brevity of life is certainly a major focus, within the Psalter the juxtaposition of Psalm 89 and Psalm 90 is significant, where the former concludes Book 3 of the Psalter and the latter begins Book 4. Psalm 89 affirms the Davidic covenant but ends on an apparent note of defeat. Psalm 90 is Mosaic and conveys a message of God's eternality and that of his purpose, thereby inferring the continuity of the covenant. See Grogan, *Psalms*, 23–24. Viewing the Psalter as a postexilic document, deClaissé-Walford concurs ("Canonical Shape of Psalms," 105–6).

31. Lioy, "Teach Us to Number Our Days," 106–7.

for us to make comparisons. Because of the historical and cultural distance between an OT character and us today, we should strive to filter the OT through the NT, located within the same historical-redemptive period as us, if possible. Fortuitously, Paul discusses Abraham specifically in Romans 4. The divine promises to Abraham are inherited by his descendants, both Jews and gentiles, when characterized by his kind of faith (Rom 4:16).

Let us take a closer look at Abraham's situation in which he demonstrates his faith. Paul recounts (Rom 4:18–22):

> In hope against hope he believed, so that he might become a father of many nations according to that which had been spoken, "So shall your descendants be." Without becoming weak in faith he contemplated his own body, now as good as dead since he was about a hundred years old, and the deadness of Sarah's womb; yet, with respect to the promise of God, he did not waver in unbelief but grew strong in faith, giving glory to God, and being fully assured that what God had promised, he was able also to perform. Therefore it was also credited to him as righteousness.

Already we are thinking, the man is 100, beyond the life span of most of us today. True. But two key observations encourage us. First, Abraham reviews his circumstance and thinks, "No way." He realizes the impossibility of childbearing since he and his wife have far exceeded the normal age to conceive. Humanly speaking, the prospect of becoming new parents lies outside their ability to contribute. They have just received God's promise of a son. Their challenge is to believe that God will accomplish the impossible in fulfillment of his own word. We cannot relate to this very situation unless we too have received a specific divine promise for which fulfillment lies beyond our ability to contribute. But in more general situations not involving such promises, have we not found ourselves in a predicament about which we lack the ability and resources to address effectively? God's intervention represents our only viable hope. Of course, since he does not commit himself to that kind of promise to us, whether he intervenes on our behalf as we hope remains uncertain. Second, Abraham's and his wife's age emerge as prominent factors contributing to their situation. Here, those of us older folks can definitely relate. Our advanced age complicates our circumstances. Things we can do earlier in life escape our ability now. Of course, in Sarah's case, she has been barren all her life. With age, however, it becomes doubly impossible to conceive.

Paul himself gives us added motivation to find Abraham's relevance in his doctrinal discussion about justification by faith.[32] But to reduce his writings to concern only for an individual's salvation is simplistic and ignores other important emphases.[33]

We find, then, Abraham and his challenge as pertinent today. Certain aspects of his story can reappear in our stories. Abraham is the father of many descendants as the prototype of faith invoking God's approval and as progenitor. As his descendants, we bear his defining characteristic—faith. God's promise to him is directly fulfilled for us as proclaimed by Paul's writings. *An immediate hermeneutical principle states that we older readers of Scripture note its narrative focus on the details of Abraham's life only begins at the age of 75 (Gen 12:4), thereby speaking to us located in our later years.* Abraham is already advanced in age when his story unfolds but the best years of his life lie ahead. We take great interest because we are part of his family; this collective identity especially resonates with us who are Asian, and because we can reorient our perspective to look forward to what lies ahead in our lives even though most of our lives has passed. We believe the Lord has something significant in store for us in our future. Reading Abraham gives us hope about our lives so that we make plans.

Another hermeneutical principle is that, when the NT confirms the correspondence between an OT character's situation and challenge and our contemporary lives, we have the opportunity to learn something from our exemplar by way of instruction, encouragement, or warning, especially when the character's age assumes an important role. We acknowledge that the historical promise to Abraham is only for him to claim. He receives it by direct revelation. For us, Scripture represents God's revelation of his will and intentions. We do not receive direct revelation. With the completion of the biblical canon, we do not expect any such communication. However, relatively speaking, we can relate to Abraham in his old age. We see ourselves as old (not as old as Abraham perhaps), our bodies not as vigorous

---

32. Although Moo argues that Christology is Paul's organizing focus in Paul's thoughts, justification by faith occupies an important role in his writings. See Moo, *Romans*, 89–91; and Iswahyudi and Putrawan, "Justification by Faith," 60–66. Stettler contends that Paul did not originate the concept, which is found earlier in Jesus' teaching of the parable of the Pharisee and tax collector in Luke 18:9–14 ("Did Paul Invent?," 161–96).

33. See, for example, Reis, "Justification by Faith," 23–41. Wright balances his understanding of Paul about each individual's response to Christ and the corporate element of Christ's body, ecclesiology (*Pauline Perspectives*, 285).

as before (maybe not as dead as Abraham's body). And, like Abraham and Sarah, we have long since passed the age of childbearing. We might press the analogy to cover other aspects of old age that makes us all too conscious of the reduction in our physical and mental capacities.

But that analogy should be exercised with caution—all the narrative and Paul tell us is that the couple does not expect to have children naturally. That expectation, however, does not necessarily imply they do not lead an active life with great responsibilities, as if they are waiting for death like some very aged and incapacitated people today. In fact, Abraham heads a substantial household with servants, possessions, and various animals (Gen 24:35, 53). In an earlier account, we learn that he has over three hundred men trained for warfare (Gen 14:14).

Chapter 3

Summarizing the Principles of the Biblical Hermeneutics of Ageism

Collecting all the major principles from the previous chapter into one convenient summary, we present them below. Every one of them has a bearing on the subject of ageism but to varying degrees. Some are more generic and so move to the background, whereas others have a greater specificity.

REVIEW OF THE PRINCIPLES

1. Covenantal stipulations are an enduring divine mandate on God's people, including the aged, spanning much of history, the covenants with Abraham and Moses to the new covenant that demand our stewardship.

2. Read Scripture as everyone else regardless of age or station in life unless the text clearly specifies an age-specific admonition.

3. In order to obey the moral law, especially as recorded in the OT, we must perform the necessary contextualization to overcome the disjunction between the OT and the NT, and between the ancient world and the modern.

4. The kind of wisdom inferred from our reading of Job that older folks should have and display is theological and spiritual; and we must pass that wisdom on to the next generation so that they too revere the Lord.

5. Identify all Messianic prophecies fulfilled in Jesus Christ as the most impactful promise we can receive.

6. Read and interpret Scripture to combat the vulnerabilities inherent with old age as a defense in spiritual warfare.

7. The possibility of finding an edifying example increases when we modern readers can compare ourselves with a biblical character living within the same historical-redemptive period as us with whom we share critical spiritual characteristics, including advanced age.

8. Regardless of personal background, whether individualistic or collectivistic, we automatically become spiritually collectivistic in Christ with the fundamental duty of loving and honoring one another within the believing community, and so read and interpret Scripture with this changed orientation.

9. If others within the believing community regard me as older, I can read and interpret Scripture as an older person in order to see how I may fulfill my role as a father or mother.

10. Even with a distinct hermeneutics of ageism, the interpretation of one's moral and spiritual responsibility to the Lord does not differentiate between the young and old. Hence, there would be no recourse for a hermeneutics of suspicion that characterizes feminist and ecological readings, as Scripture does not evidence a bias against the aged.

11. We must discern the difference between what is unique, not to be emulated, and what can serve as a model for today.

12. The hermeneutical principle of scalability features two parts: first, separate out a biblical character's abilities and narrative role that can exceed our own talents and differ from our stewardship as not something to emulate, except possibly on a more limited scale; and second, strive to emulate the admirable virtues that characterize them as what God expects from us.

13. Regarding the characters' mentioned ages as a theological benchmark, we offer a hermeneutical principle: characters' ages and progressive aging serve as a narrative time marker to give readers the sense of God's faithfulness to his promises and of the gradual unfolding of his plans over the years.

14. The narrative and its emphasis are the determinative factors for discerning whether a character's recorded age plays an important role in the story or not. A corollary principle suggests that, even if a character's age does not play an explicit role in the narrative, it may still offer valuable insights on a person's character trait so long as readers do not subvert the narrative's major points.

15. Interpret all moral and ethical demands as continually relevant throughout all of life to the very end.

16. The hermeneutical principles of the urgent and of the continual relevance of our moral and ethical responsibilities throughout our lives to the very end represent our stewardship as we read and meditate on Scripture.

17. We older readers of Scripture note its narrative focus on the details of Abraham's life only begins at the age of 75 (Gen 12:4), thereby speaking to us located in our later years as we read about Abraham.

18. When the NT confirms the correspondence between an OT character's situation and challenge and our contemporary lives, we have the opportunity to learn something from our exemplar by way of instruction, encouragement, or warning, especially when the character's age assumes an important role.

PRINCIPLES SPECIFICALLY RELATED TO AGEISM

I now reduce the list by retaining only those that deal specifically with ageism, rewording the principle for greater clarity. The others, while still important, do not differ from general hermeneutical principles covered in the standard literature.

a. Read and interpret Scripture as anyone else regardless of age or station in life unless the text specifies an age-specific admonition.

b. Even with a distinct hermeneutics of ageism, the interpretation of one's moral and spiritual responsibility to the Lord does not differentiate between the young and old. Hence, there would be no recourse to a hermeneutics of suspicion that characterizes feminist and ecological readings, as Scripture does not evidence a bias against the aged.

c. Read and interpret Scripture to resist the Adversary in spiritual warfare, giving particular attention to the vulnerabilities inherent with old age.

d. If the believing community regards a member as older, that member should read and interpret Scripture to see how they may fulfill their role as a "father" or "mother," thereby leaving a legacy. The kind of wisdom (inferred from reading Job) that older folks should have and display is theological and spiritual; and we must pass that wisdom on to the next generation so that they too revere the Lord.

e. Interpret the biblical characters' explicitly mentioned progression in age as a theological benchmark. The characters' ages and progressive aging serve as a narrative time marker to give readers the sense of God's faithfulness to his promises and of the gradual unfolding of his plans over the years.

f. The narrative and its emphasis are the determinative factors for discerning whether a character's recorded age plays an important role in the story or not. Even if a character's age does not play an important role in the narrative, it may still offer valuable insights into a person's character trait (for example, faithfulness over the years) so long as the reader does not subvert the narrative's major points in such character studies.

g. The hermeneutical principles of the urgent, fueled by an older person's sense that their remaining time is fast dwindling, and of the continual relevance of their moral and ethical responsibilities to the very end inform their reading and interpreting Scripture.

h. Regarding Abraham specifically, older readers note that Scripture's narrative focus on the details of his life only begins at the age of 75 (Gen 12:4). Thus, his story may speak to them located in their later years. A similar focus on Moses's life and service begins at the burning bush (Exod 3:1–2) when he is 80 (Exod 7:7).

IMPRESSIONS

In this investigation for possible age-related interpretative issues, the Scriptures give the overriding impression that the young and old within the covenant community hold equal status and accountability. Paul famously states (Gal 3:28): "There is neither Jew nor Greek, there is neither slave nor free, there is neither male nor female; for you are all one in Christ Jesus." We can easily add: "There is neither young nor old; for we are all one in Christ Jesus."

Usually, the age of a biblical character, when recorded, serves the narrative function in highlighting a theological or christological point being made. The age progression of prominent figures like Abraham, Jacob, Joseph, Moses, and David in the OT and Paul, to a certain extent in the NT, provides a marker to note the time progression through which God's promises and agenda are fulfilled. Consequently, a strong sense of his sovereign authority emerges with the depiction of his lordship in history over peoples and nations, often transcending the normal boundaries of human life spans. Scripture marks Daniel's age by the kings under whom he serves, leaving readers the task of estimating his age at each important stage of his career. These individuals living rather long lives testify to God using them in strategic ways, reinforcing the impression that such lengthy careers have less to do with fortuitous longevity genes and more about God choosing them for their roles that require significant time periods.

The list of OT exemplars of faith in Hebrews 11 spans from the dawn of human history in Abel's story down through the rest of the OT to speak to readers of the NT period. The passage omits the ages of these exemplars. God is the common denominator throughout as the object of their faith. The omission of age suggests that, regardless of our age or stage in life, our most critical attribute is faith or belief, specifically in the divine promises, and not our age. Age, then, does not handicap us nor should we use it as an excuse not to trust God and obey his word. That realization should motivate us older readers as God can and will continue to demand our allegiance and service to him up to the very end. May this description fit us well: "All these died in faith, without receiving the promises, but having seen and welcomed them from a distance, and having confessed that they were strangers and exiles on the earth" (Heb 11:13).

CHAPTER 4

Specific Scriptural References to Old Age

A REVIEW OF SOME scriptural references to old age provides a biblical perspective. However, we may hesitate to cover Abraham, Isaac, or Jacob even if they are prominent in Bible history, particularly Abraham. One primary reason lies in their respective life spans—Abraham lives until 175 (Gen 25:7), Isaac to 180 (Gen 35:28), and Jacob to 147 (Gen 47:28)—which, from our modern perspective, seems too legendary to be realistic and to which we cannot relate. Even Joseph, who lives for 110 years (Gen 50:22, 26), lies beyond most of us. Another reason for our hesitation is that they all are strategic in God's plan spanning the ages. They remain active to varying degrees in the lives of their families until the end. Jacob, for example, blesses his sons with a prophecy about the future for each one, although he is bedridden and about to die (Gen 49:1–28). Joseph has some final words for his brothers especially about God's promise to their forefathers (Gen 50:24).

MOSES AND AARON, A PAIR OF OCTOGENARIANS

If, however, we take a snapshot of Moses and Aaron at the time God sends them to confront Pharaoh, the text informs us that they are 80 and 83, respectively (Exod 7:7). We stand a better chance relating to and learning from them than in their later career in the wilderness. Yet, we may view their strategic role as God's agents of delivering Israel out of Egyptian bondage as way beyond anything we can aspire to accomplish at a comparable age. Moses performs miraculous wonders in executing the series of plagues against the Egyptians, something no one else would ever replicate (compare Deut 34:10–12). But we recognize his abilities as God-given in order for God to magnify himself before Pharaoh and to make a name for himself before the nations later (for example, Josh 2:9–11, where Rahab recounts God drying up the Red Sea and defeating the Amorites). Instead, we focus on Moses and Aaron as men.

In this regard, both men "as the Lord commanded them, so they did" (Exod 7:6b). We can relate to their faith and obedience to the Lord. We can also relate to Moses's struggle at the beginning when God first appears to him at the burning bush (Exod 3:1—4:17). He actually rejects God selecting him to lead Israel out of Egypt in spite of a demonstration of the two signs with the staff becoming a snake and the hand turning leprous. In claiming a lack of speaking ability, he incurs God's anger, but God accommodates Moses's reservation by recruiting Aaron as spokesperson. In this manner, Moses reveals his innate humanity. Have we not tried the Lord's patience when we hesitate or disobey? Have we not expressed doubt in our abilities? And have we, like Moses, not experienced God's patience and accommodation?

Yet, we marvel at the two men's physical vigor during their battle of wills and wits against a likely younger pharaoh. The narrative gives no hint of them struggling with fatigue. Given the tendency of biblical narrative to mentioning only what is pertinent to the main theme of the passage, however, any asides not contributing to that focus would be omitted. Moses and Aaron are not discouraged, fearful, or doubtful during this ordeal. They persevere. Even though we can relate to Moses's initial hesitancy and find encouragement from his later faithful obedience to the Lord, we may still struggle avoiding intimidation to Moses's herculean task of confronting a staunch opponent in pharaoh and his people and leading a nation-sized contingent out of bondage to a somewhat uncertain future in our reading. After all, our reading agenda is to discern relatable aspects of Moses's and Aaron's activities and, at the same time, avoid mistakenly thinking that God may call us to high-profile tasks like saving an entire nation.

Significantly, Moses is the most humble man on earth (Num 12:3). Is that a key trait that God notes and hence calls Moses to a very important mission? Humility is not age specific. It should characterize the young or the old and anyone given a critical task to complete. Humility drives a person to total dependence on God's grace and wisdom and to redirect any accolade to him. Moses exemplifies that. In response to Miriam's and Aaron's challenge of Moses's authority as God's spokesperson, God distinguishes

Moses from all other prophets as someone to whom he speaks face to face clearly and not through enigmatic riddles (Num 12:1–8). And when God afflicts Miriam with leprosy as a consequence, Moses urgently appeals to God to heal her. From this episode we see Moses exemplifying the oft-repeated adage, "Whoever exalts himself shall be humbled, and whoever humbles himself shall be exalted" (Matt 23:12; Luke 14:11; 18:14). A somewhat similar principle states, "The proud look of humanity will be brought low, and the arrogance of people will be humbled; and the Lord alone will be exalted on that day" (Isa 2:11). Later, Jesus himself displays this trait as crucial for his mission (Matt 11:29; Phil 2:8). Hence, even in our old age, we remain humble, not because of lowered capabilities but in order that we make ourselves available for the Lord's use and, in due time, he may honor us. Cannot God use anyone for his service? Let us not make excuses like Moses. Let us instead believe that God can and will use us even in old age.

GIDEON, LONGTIME JUDGE

After defeating the invading Midianite army, Gideon declines the Israelites' request that he rule over them and states, instead, that the Lord is ruler (Judg 8:22–23). Unfortunately, he misleads the people in worshiping the golden ephod he constructs (Judg 8:27). However, he serves as judge for some unspecified time even though the narrative mentions forty years of peace in his lifetime (Judg 8:28). Following his death at an old age (Judg 8:32), Israel immediately returns to Baal worship (Judg 8:33), implying, it seems, that Gideon continues to exert an influence over the people throughout his life. These brief comments depict at least a semi-active role for him in the remaining years of his life after the victory over Midian.

BARZILLAI, A VERY OLD MAN

The pertinent passage (2 Sam 19:32–37a) records the moment:

> Barzillai was very old: eighty years old; and he had provided the king food while he stayed in Mahanaim, for he was a very great man. So the king said to Barzillai, "You cross over with me, and I will provide you food in Jerusalem with me." But Barzillai said to the king, "How long do I still have to live, that I should go up with the king to Jerusalem? I am now eighty years old. Can I distinguish between good and bad? Or can your servant taste what I eat or

what I drink? Or can I still hear the voice of men and women singing? Why then should your servant be an added burden to my lord the king? Your servant would merely cross over the Jordan with the king. So why should the king compensate me with this reward? Please let your servant return, so that I may die in my own city near the grave of my father and my mother."

After the death of Absalom, who nearly topples David from the throne, the king returns to Jerusalem triumphantly. Barzillai plays a key role in offering safe refuge. In gratitude the king invites him to return and enjoy the provisions of a court life. But Barzillai declines citing his advanced age for not going. He can no longer enjoy the pleasures of life, good food and entertainment. He lost his sense of taste and his hearing has deteriorated significantly. The only prospect for the future is his impending death. In spite of the king's gracious offer, Barzillai would only be a burden, needing special care.

We older folks can relate all too well. We don't want to be a grievous burden to our families and the simple pleasures of life may lie beyond our reach. So, our realistic prospect is our impending end. Indeed, years ago when I was much younger, I would sometimes converse with the senior contingent of our Chinese American church, people well into their eighties and beyond. One enterprising senior lady informs me that she regularly plays mahjong, often by herself. She does it not so much for fun and relaxation but to keep her mind sharp as the game requires strategy. She claims it is an effective deterrent against senility. But several other seniors simply state that their days are spent waiting to die. It seems morbid to me at the time. How sad and pathetic. Life holds no hope for meaning and significance other than death? No plans, even simple and short-term ones? Do they in some sense stop living?

Barzillai, for example, has recently hosted David and his sizable entourage until the danger passes. The logistics and supplies must be substantial. Overseeing the entire operation and caring for so many people demand of Barzillai leadership, planning, organizational and supply chain skills, and hospitality. He may be very old but he is still very capable, at least short-term. Of course, the exigency of the moment prompts an adrenaline rush. Thus, even though very old, Barzillai can still rise to the occasion and admirably so.

We conjecture that Barzillai does not do all the work as host. Given the size of David's entourage, we assume that Barzillai heads a large household including servants who do the actual labor. *His situation recalls a Filipino household, often featuring several generations, where the oldest member enjoys great respect and exercises authority in decision-making matters, having the final say. Being wealthy, Barzillai's army of servants finds a pale analogy in some Asian households, particularly in Singapore and Hong Kong, with domestic workers. Wealthy families, however, may hire a chauffeur, personal secretary or assistant, several maids, a babysitter for very young children, and a cook.*

In the narrative flow, Barzillai contributes to facilitating God's plan for David. David will continue as king, overcoming the temporary challenge of his son to usurp the throne. Absalom cannot succeed, as God does not remove his love from David as from Saul. Barzillai, then, serves a brief but important role of preservation. God expresses his faithfulness to David through Barzillai.

This episode, however, spurs us to take stock of our present capabilities and ask ourselves, Would we be able to rise to the occasion should the situation demand it? Would we be alert in looking around to see if anyone might benefit from our participation in some way, even to a limited degree? What are the needs around us? Asking these questions challenges us to have the attitude that we can still be of value to someone regardless of age and personal limitations.

These questions would not even be asked in Asia. In rural areas, for example, the elderly of the Kachin tribes of northwest Myanmar enjoy active engagement in the village and at home. Their families and even the community seek their advice and guidance, having great respect for their wisdom. The same is true among Filipinos who habitually consult the elderly before making decisions. Indeed, the patriarch or matriarch has the final say.

Like Barzillai, we may serve a narrative role, briefly or more lengthy, in fulfilling God's plan and purpose. Being older, should we not possess the necessary discernment in order to ascertain how we may continue to serve our Lord? Does he not include us in the pursuit of his agenda? Scripture does not support the concept of retirement from the Lord's service. So long as we continue in this life, we may safely assume God has something in mind for us.

CALEB AND JOSHUA, OLD BUT VIGOROUS MEN

Unlike Barzillai, Caleb and Joshua at the time of the conquest still enjoy the vigor and strength of a younger man and so assume a leading role in taking possession of the promised land. Their significance and leading role fulfill God's promise that they will enter the land in sharp contrast to their fellow spies and generation (Num 14:22–24). Their advanced age and vigor are not so much a testament to their uncommon health and strength but confirmation of the Lord's word about them. Their key trait is belief in God in sad contrast to all the others who die in the wilderness. Caleb states (Josh 14:7–12):

> I was forty years old when Moses the servant of the Lord sent me from Kadesh-barnea to spy out the land, and I brought word back to him as it was in my heart. Nevertheless my brothers who went up with me made the heart of the people melt with fear; but I followed the Lord my God fully. So Moses swore on that day, saying, "The land on which your foot has walked shall certainly be an inheritance to you and to your children forever, because you have followed the Lord my God fully." And now behold, the Lord has let me live, just as he spoke, these forty-five years, from the time that the Lord spoke this word to Moses, when Israel walked in the wilderness; and now behold, I am eighty-five years old today. I am still as strong today as I was on the day Moses sent me; as my strength was then, so my strength is now, for war and for going out and coming in. Now then, give me this hill country about which the Lord spoke on that day, for you heard on that day that Anakim were there, with great fortified cities; perhaps the Lord will be with me, and I will drive them out just as the Lord has spoken.

Amazingly Caleb is older than Barzillai, being 85 years old, but affirms his physical prowess and fitness to challenge the Anakites, a formidable foe. Caleb is not self-deluded but offers an accurate self-appraisal. His faith, courage, fighting skills, and strength remain strong. In view of the circumstances of taking the land and in fulfillment of God's promise to Caleb personally, Caleb may well be the exception. Similarly, we may assume that Joshua too is of a similar age and equally vigorous as he has the God-given task of leading the twelve tribes to conquest. Both men are God's agents to accomplish his intention of bringing his people into the land first promised to Abraham (Gen 12:1, 5; 15:7, 16, 18–21; 17:8). Hence, we conclude that God circumvents the natural processes, including aging and its attendant negative effects, in order to move his agenda forward through these two men.

Still later toward the end of the conquest, the narrative states that Joshua is old (Josh 23:1). He summons the leaders of Israel to exhort them to remain strong and faithful to the Lord and to warn them against mingling with the survivors of nations which are driven out (Josh 23:3–16). Israel's prosperity depends on their continued allegiance to the Lord, otherwise they would perish quickly. Then Joshua summons all the Israelites to Shechem for him to review with them their history from the days of Abraham and his father through the period in Egypt and in the wilderness to victories over the Amorites (Josh 24:2–13). This review testifies to God's powerful intervention on their behalf, setting the stage for Joshua's challenge to them to serve the Lord with the warning of dire consequences for failure to do so (Josh 24:14–24). Finally, Joshua makes a covenant with the people to reaffirm the decrees and laws (Josh 24:25–27). Although quite old at this point, Joshua still functions as Israel's undisputed leader and exerts a strong moral and spiritual influence on them as confirmed by the narrator's epitaph: "Israel served the Lord throughout the lifetime of Joshua" (Josh 24:31a).

Caleb and Joshua are unique, certainly not typical of people their age. The overriding story of God's covenant promise of the land to his people and him keeping that promise serve as the dramatic backdrop for both men's strategic roles. It is not too farfetched to surmise that God supernaturally extends their careers in order to help situate Israel in the land as a nation among the community of nations. Perhaps the most we may extract from their stories is that we can still serve the Lord in some meaningful way even in our later years so long as we follow the Lord our God wholeheartedly. We cannot boast with Caleb that we are as vigorous as we once were several decades ago. But we should not be waiting to die either, thinking that our remaining days are empty. We can still plan. However, like any plan at any age, it depends on the Lord.

Yet, the biggest point we can draw from Caleb and Joshua may be separated into two related thoughts. First, we must follow the Lord wholeheartedly throughout all our lives even into old age. There is never a time when our fervor for him should diminish. Although our physical vigor may lessen, our moral and spiritual vigor should remain ever strong. Indeed, with the length of years of having followed and served the Lord, our faith should grow stronger. Second, we can still exert a moral and spiritual influence on others, particularly the young. Our faithfulness, perseverance, and steadfast integrity provide for us a credibility that is unshakable and a voice that warrants a hearing. We serve as a role model when we can echo Joshua: "But as for me and my house, we will serve the Lord" (Josh 24:15d).

In regard to exercising influence on the family, Asian culture facilitates a platform as family members hold the elderly in high regard, deferring to their judgment. Eagerly sought, their wisdom finds a receptive audience with the younger set. They can leverage their position to model devotion to God and an upright character worthy of imitation. Thus, they can bless their household and so quote Joshua authoritatively.

If we should find it difficult to relate to Caleb and Joshua in the vigor and significant accomplishments in their advanced ages, Moses would pose an even greater challenge for us as he continues leading Israel until he is 120 years old (Deut 31:2). Even at that stage in life his eyesight and strength remain unabated (Deut 34:7). Theoretically, had he not failed to uphold the Lord's holiness, he would have been the one to lead the nation into the promised land to possess it (compare Deut 32:48–52). But as the closing narrative of Deut 34:10–12 affirms, no other prophet can compare with Moses in the mode of communication with the Lord and the power he displays in performing astounding miraculous signs.

Yet, we might extract a warning based on Moses's life and career. Can we suffer a similar termination of our service to the Lord if we, like Moses, fail the Lord in some significant manner? No one is indispensable. As God raises up Joshua to replace Moses so too the Lord can replace any one of us. Let us, then, be ever vigilant to safeguard our attitude and conduct in order not to become a stumbling block to others.

DAVID, RULER FOR MANY YEARS

According to 2 Sam 5:4, David becomes king at 30 years of age and rules for forty years. Thus, when 1 Kgs 1:1 describes him as very old and he cannot stay warm, he must be approaching 70. Before he dies (1 Kgs 2:10), however, he has his son Solomon anointed king to succeed him (1 Kgs 1:39). With his mental faculties still functional, David instructs his loyal servants, including Zadok the priest who pours oil on Solomon, on the coronation procedure, which they carry out (1 Kgs 1:32–40). Then shortly later as he senses the end coming, David charges Solomon to tidy up some loose ends that can potentially mean trouble for his reign if not properly dealt with

(1 Kgs 2:1–9). Heeding his father's advice, Solomon quickly establishes his rule (1 Kgs 2:22–46). Even though David hands over his rule to his son before his death, David uses the little time left in life to ensure his son's rule will be secure. Hence, using contemporary parlance, we might regard Solomon as the king and his father David as king emeritus. He exerts influence over the new king like a mentor or advisor.

Strictly speaking, David does not retire. Rather, he expedites his son's coronation quickly in order to preempt his other son's attempt to usurp the throne (1 Kgs 1:5–10). Up to the day of his death, it seems, David oversees the transition of kingship in an orderly and peaceful manner to ensure that the rightful successor is installed.

The succession between kings marks the major narrative of David's story. What merits some attention is his family's story where his failure as a father would have derailed the main storyline if his son Absalom's conspiracy to dethrone him succeeded. Earlier, David remains passively silent, although angry, at Amnon's violation of Tamar, two of his children (2 Sam 13:1–21). As the father, David should have acted but he does not. Consequently, Absalom, Tamar's full brother, exacts revenge later, then flees (2 Sam 13:34). Again, David takes no action to bring Absalom back until Joab intervenes (2 Sam 13:38–39; 14:1–33). These events may well pave the way for Absalom's conspiracy. The overarching narrative depicts God's faithfulness to his covenant promise to David in defusing Absalom's threat. *But Asian readers notice the family tragedy that clearly portrays David's inept parenting. The head of an Asian household normally commands the respect and allegiance of the family; he sets the ground rules for family values and conduct.* We wonder if any of his sons really respect him. Amnon easily deceives him into having Tamar come (2 Sam 13:6–8). *This deception shows disrespect, a severe violation of Asian cultural values.* Tamar's rape by her own brother brings great dishonor upon the family. Children are expected to uphold the family honor. But Amnon fails miserably. David is further dishonored and humiliated as he must vacate the throne and flee from Absalom.

DANIEL, LONG CAREER IN CIVIL SERVICE

Since I already covered Daniel in a previous chapter, I will not do so here again other than to note that his story belongs here as well. Except for the occasional vision that he interprets, most of his career is administration—a stewardship that he carries out with excellence and faithfulness. His consistently outstanding performance rating pushes him to the forefront where the king plans to give him charge over the whole kingdom (Dan 6:1–3). This is a great public honor. Unfortunately for him, however, jealousy and resentment on the part of the other administrators and satraps provoke a conspiracy to eliminate him (Dan 6:4–15), and they nearly succeed when he is thrown into the lions' den (Dan 6:16–18).[1] But God protects Daniel, which prompts the king to publicly revere Daniel's God (Dan 6:19–27). The connection between Daniel's exceptional service and God's glory is dramatically highlighted. In this incidence, God and Daniel are honored, God through his life-preserving intervention and Daniel vindicated by surviving the night. His lengthy civil service career forms the backbone for his interpretation of the occasional dream or vision by a king, spaced over the years. He is ever available to serve either administratively or interpretively. Insightfully, we find that Daniel acquires honor through his faithful civil service over the decades (Dan 1:21) as well as through his ability to interpret dreams and visions. Both ways are important even though his interpretative activity is more spectacular.

PAUL, THE AGED

Scripture does not provide sufficient information to estimate Paul's life span. Thus, we cannot calculate with confidence how old he is at death. However, writings by the early church fathers offer some idea but the historical accuracy of their accounts remains tenuous.

Clement of Rome, the leader of the church at Rome, lived in the latter part of the first century of the Christian era. In his first epistle to the Corinthian church, he seems to have inferred Paul's martyrdom (5:5–6):

> By reason of jealousy and strife Paul by his example pointed out the prize of patient endurance. After that he had been seven times in bonds, had been driven into exile, had been stoned, had preached in the East and in the West, he won the noble renown which was the reward of his faith, having taught righteousness unto the whole world and having reached the farthest bounds of the West; and when he had borne his testimony before the rulers,

---

1. According to Malina, acquiring honor can provoke a contest with competitors and for Daniel it nearly costs him his life (*New Testament World*, 52). But unlike ancient contests, Daniel simply trusts in God and does not attempt to oppose his challengers.

so he departed from the world and went unto the holy place, having been found a notable pattern of patient endurance.[2]

Clement's reference that Paul "departed from the world and went unto the holy place" seems to imply his death. But his description of Paul's fate is too vague to prove conclusive. In the fourth century of the Christian era, Eusebius of Caesarea, a Greek historian and biblical exegete compiles his *Ecclesiastical History* in which he states explicitly both Paul's and Peter's martyrdom during Nero's reign. In book 2, chapter 25, Eusebius writes:

> Thus publicly announcing himself as the first among God's chief enemies, he was led on to the slaughter of the apostles. It is, therefore, recorded that Paul was beheaded in Rome itself, and that Peter likewise was crucified under Nero. This account of Peter and Paul is substantiated by the fact that their names are preserved in the cemeteries of that place even to the present day.[3]

We may correlate Paul's death with the great fire of Rome when Nero accuses Christians of starting the fire in order to divert suspicion from himself, assuming Eusebius's accuracy.[4] That locates Paul's demise in the year 64 of the Christian era. That date, however, may be too precise. Establishing a chronology of Paul's life represents a tentative effort due to the lack of hard evidence outside of the Scriptures. Consequently, one scholar offers a range of dates for Paul's birth and death, between 5 BCE and 10 CE for his birth and between 62 CE and 68 CE for his death.[5] Thus, Paul dies at an age ranging from his early fifties to his early seventies. His is an unnatural death and so we may safely conclude that he does not die of old age. Yet, we wonder about the quality of life toward his end.

From his final letter, we conclude that Paul clearly anticipates his end (2 Tim 4:6–8). Confidently, he affirms that he has maintained faithfulness to the stewardship entrusted to him. He has finished his course and now awaits his reward. He harbors no regrets, only certainty that he has completed his mission. At the time of this letter, he is in prison (2 Tim 1:8, 12) and abandoned by a fair number of people (2 Tim 1:15; 4:10, 16) but not completely (2 Tim 1:16–17; 4:11, 21b). He still manages to care for Timothy

2. Lightfoot, "First Epistle of Clement to Corinthians."
3. Eusebius of Caesarea, *Church History*, §2.25.
4. Champlin, *Nero*, 121.
5. Gorman, *Apostle of the Crucified Lord*, 44–45.

and to offer him some final advice with this letter. And he continues steadfast against his adversaries (2 Tim 4:14) in order to proclaim his message to a broad range of gentiles with the Lord by his side (2 Tim 4:17). Recalling Daniel's experience, Paul writes (2 Tim 4:17d), "I was rescued out of the lion's mouth." Yet, he thinks he still has some time left as he instructs Timothy to visit him with a cloak and his scrolls, especially his parchments (2 Tim 4:9, 13).

However old Paul is at this juncture, he still has sufficient strength and fervor to endure imprisonment, abandonment, and adversaries. Physically, emotionally, mentally, and spiritually, Paul continues strong and unbowed. He credits the Lord for his effective ministry, protection, and eventual entry into the heavenly kingdom (2 Tim 4:18).

From Paul's final letter and his expressed intentions, we infer that he fully dedicates his life to his ministry. His life course would only conclude when the Lord takes him to his eternal home. Until then, he continues proclaiming the message. He does not let imprisonment or abandonment deter his efforts. His resolve remains unshakable. If anything, it seems, his resolve empowers him to continue to the very end of his life. The Lord's intervention plays a significant part as well.

Based on our investigation of Paul, we extract a few thoughts. First, the other people we examined (Caleb, Joshua, and Daniel) remain faithful to their respective God-given responsibilities and God's blessings and intervention are clearly seen where, in Daniel's case, God's work effectively moves powerful gentile kings to acknowledge him publicly. Paul's life and ministry likewise showcase God's presence in sometimes miraculous ways. Paul also proves faithful to the end. Old age does not deter or weaken their resolve to serve. Given only the isolated episode of Barzillai granting David and his people refuge for a period of time and without any background on the man, we cannot say that Barzillai follows the pattern evident in the others we have studied. However, we can conclude that Barzillai plays a very vital role of sustaining David to protect him and to facilitate fulfillment of God's promise of him becoming the next king. Barzillai carries out this important service when he is 80. Again, old age does not prevent him from serving David, even though he has to decline the king's invitation to go to Jerusalem.

Second, none of the men retires in our sense of the concept. No hint of leisurely time spent nor of a subsequent career (for example, I know of a number of former civil servants who retire from the government and then

Specific Scriptural References to Old Age

accept a paid position, often as a consultant) emerge from their respective stories. Of the men surveyed, Barzillai comes closest to our understanding about retirement. Barzillai declines David's invitation to go to Jerusalem in order to enjoy the king's hospitality. Barzillai desires, instead, to live out the remainder of his days in his hometown near the burial site of his parents (2 Sam 19:37a). We presume he would then lead a quiet life of relative inactivity, waiting for the end.

Third, all the men who serve the Lord until the very end appear to discern that their service would continue until the end. No clue, however, is given as to how they know. In fact, in his farewell address to the Ephesian elders (Acts 20:22–25), Paul states that he does not know his future in detail other than imprisonment and hardship and the certainty of not seeing the elders again. However, his ambition is: "But I do not consider my life of any account as dear to myself, so that I may finish my course and the ministry which I received from the Lord Jesus, to testify solemnly of the gospel of God's grace" (Acts 20:24). He may suspect that his race will terminate with his death. But he is willing to sacrifice his life if required. We suspect that attitude characterizes Caleb, Joshua, and Daniel too.

But we have one clear example in Moses. As soon as he blesses the tribes of Israel (Deut 33:1–29), Moses climbs Mount Nebo from the top of which God shows him the promised land (Deut 34:1–4). Then immediately he dies (Deut 34:5). To his very last day of life, Moses prophesies and leads his people. Only after his death does Joshua assume the mantle of leadership (Deut 34:9). And if tradition proves accurate, Paul and Peter continue as apostles until their martyrdom. Joshua's case remains unclear. We do not know the time differential between him dismissing the people to take possession of their inheritance as his final duty as their leader (Josh 24:28) and his death (Josh 24:29). Even if some time transpires between the two events, we can easily picture Joshua busily taking possession of his own inheritance—clearing and cultivating the land and building his home. And, as the spiritual leader of his own family, he would ensure that his entire household remains faithful to the Lord (Josh 24:15d). Likely, Caleb finishes out his days in a similar fashion as Joshua, although he has to drive out the Anakites and the inhabitants of Debir (Josh 15:13–17).

Several of our Chinese American friends represent a modern analogy to Joshua's continued family responsibility after completing his duty of leading the conquest. Upon retirement from their corporate careers, they transition into full-time grandparenting in helping to raise their grandchildren while the parents go to work. Every workday from morning until evening and sometimes overnight they care for the youngsters, feeding, playing, teaching, and taking them for outings. They eagerly accept this responsibility. In this manner, they approximate families in Asia where deep bonds form between the elderly and the young.

TWO OLD SERVANTS, SIMEON AND ANNA

God preserves two old servants long enough in order for them to see the Christ child at his consecration (Luke 2:25–38). We are only informed that Simeon is righteous and devout. The Holy Spirit assures him that he will live to see the Messiah, the consolation of Israel. Even though the narrative does not specify his age, the fact that the Spirit promises him suggests that he is very old and will soon die. Holding the child in his arms, Simeon praises God and prophesies that the child represents God's salvation and that he is a light for the revelation to the gentiles and the glory of Israel. He continues with a disturbing prediction to Mary the mother about the child's destiny. The child will face opposition but the secrets of many hearts would be exposed. Mary herself would suffer as a result. After the fulfillment of the Spirit's promise, Simeon is now ready to die in peace.

Although not in the same league with Simeon's expectation before death, I recall two incidences with elderly Asians harboring one ambition before the end—an old grandfather wanting to see his grandson marry and my own grandmother making the arduous journey to witness my wedding despite her ailments. Both have female grandchildren but their marriages do not carry the same significance. The preferential regard for sons and grandsons characterizes both old people. In fact, my grandmother declares an unwillingness to make any effort to attend her granddaughter's wedding should that occur.

The prophetess Anna, on the other hand, is explicitly stated to be 84 years old having lived as a widow for many years. She stays in the temple continuously worshiping with fasting and prayer. She prophesies that the child will be the redemption of Jerusalem. After her brief appearance, we may presume that she continues doing what she has been doing all those years in the temple until the day of her death. Unlike for Simeon no hint suggests an imminent end for her. And there is no hint of diminished fervor or of slacking off her spiritual practices in the temple. We readers derive from the text the impression that Anna will continue strong until the Lord calls her home.

Specific Scriptural References to Old Age

Both Simeon and Anna leave us a standard of faithfulness, undiminished fervor, and clear insight into the things of the Lord. At this very late stage in life both pronounce significant prophecies about the Messiah, preserved in Scripture for later generations to read and to confirm as true on reading the rest of the Gospel according to Luke. In a sense, they participate in ushering in the First Advent, the coming of Christ in fulfillment of prophecies. Unlike the prophets of old, Simeon and Anna see with their own eyes and Simeon holds in his arms the promised redemption of their people. They straddle two ages, the former age of looking forward to God's salvation of humanity and the following age of fulfillment when God's redemption is at hand. Thus, Simeon and Anna witness the advent of the kingdom of God with Jesus' birth. They remind us of Moses standing on the top of Pisgah in Moab to survey the promised land (Deut 34:1–4). Moses sees the future but is not permitted to enter. Simeon and Anna too see the future in the Christ child, prophesy about it but, we presume, do not live long enough to see the child grow into adulthood and initiate his public ministry.

God privileges these two aged servants of God to participate in a momentous period of redemptive history. Does their story encourage us who are aged to consider what God may have in store for us? Our role most likely will not be as profound and strategic but we can still be important. Do our fervor and faithfulness remain steadfast? Can we discern our respective roles and obediently fulfill them? Until the Lord calls us home, may we pursue completing our responsibilities for the kingdom's sake.

SCRIPTURAL REFERENCES TO THE AGED

In this section we survey Scripture that refers to the aged. The first verse comes from Lev 19:32 in the form of a command: "You shall stand up in the presence of the grayheaded and honor elders, and you shall fear your God; I am the Lord." We can make three observations: (1) this admonition transcends time and culture, to be relevant and applicable at all times; (2) a visible show of respect is given by standing up, not merely an inner attitude but also an outward physical gesture; and (3) revering God closely relates to respecting the elderly. Even though embedded in the Mosaic Law, this regulation features nothing that would confine it to a particular point in history or to a particular culture. Visible expressions of respect remove any doubt in anyone's mind as to the attitude of deference toward the elderly, whether the elderly themselves or anyone else who witnesses the gesture. It is public. The most surprising aspect of this command finds God connecting his own demand for reverence toward himself and respect to the elderly. An immediate implication comes to mind: failure to respect the elderly signifies irreverence toward God.

This realization prompts us to look for other Bible references of the relationship of God and the elderly. Proverbs 30:17 states: "The eye that mocks a father and scorns a mother, the ravens of the valley will pick it out, and the young eagles will eat it."[6] The parallelism places a father and mother on the same level and they are regarded collectively, requiring due respect for both. The severe consequences of disrespecting parents cannot be easily ignored. Although this verse does not specify their age, we may presume that the admonition covers aged parents as well.

As Christians we take Scripture seriously and strive to honor our God and, if honoring the elderly is the prescribed manner to achieve that objective, then we are more than motivated to honor them as an important means of expressing our devotion to the Lord. *Reinforcing that mandate, we Asians have the added cultural tradition and practice to show reverence for the elderly. We have a double motivation through Scripture and culture. Whereas Christians raised in a non-Asian individualistic society may begin to show deference to the old upon entering into the faith, other believers from Asian collectivistic traditions have a head-start.*

In mocking Babylon's idols that need to be carried around, God contrasts himself with them by recalling how he has carried his people throughout history (Isa 46:1–7). He exhorts them (Isa 46:3–4): "Listen to me, house of Jacob, and all the remnant of the house of Israel, you who have been carried by me from birth and have been carried from the womb; even to your old age I will be the same, and even to your graying years I will carry you! I have done it, and I will bear you; and I will carry you and I will save you." From their birth to old age, Judah experiences God's faithful care and benevolence. This particular reference alludes to God's committed care throughout his people's history, a care that spans birth to old age, that is, lifelong.

In pronouncing judgment against Babylon, God declares (Isa 47:6): "I was angry with my people, I profaned my heritage and handed them over to you. You did not show mercy to them, on the aged you made your

---

6. Waltke's translation; but he shows openness to rendering "gray hair" as "old age" following the LXX (*Proverbs, Chapters 15–31*, 459–60n49).

Specific Scriptural References to Old Age

yoke very heavy." God uses Babylon to chastise his wayward people but the Babylonians prove overly cruel in afflicting the Israelites. God intends only a certain amount of suffering to discipline his people but Babylon goes beyond his intentions. Pride leads to Babylon's ruin and eventual destruction (Isa 47:7–15). In his rebuke, God cites cruelty against the aged as an especially telling evidence against the accused. This mention signifies that the elderly seem to hold a special place in God's view.

These passages should give us older readers a strong sense of importance before the Lord, seemingly even more so than others. If we feel marginalized by the younger generation or struggle to stay relevant in society, especially after retirement, Scripture nurtures our self-esteem and innate sense of worth by reminding us of God's regard for us. We derive our identity and place from him. If people depreciate us, we can ignore the slight by keeping our focus on God and seeking his approval. *But in Asian societies with strong family values, the elderly are highly esteemed, involved in family matters including decision-making.*

Chapter 5

Old Age according to the Wisdom Literature

I BELIEVE THE TOPIC of old age in the wisdom literature, especially the wisdom of Qohelet, the writer of Ecclesiastes, merits a separate treatment. The characters and their traits in the previous chapter typically assume a secondary importance compared to the theological or christological emphasis of the associated passages covered. Hopefully, I extracted meaningful insights about the characters without unduly sacrificing the passages' main thrust. However, the books of Job and especially Ecclesiastes offer an extended perspective of the aged themselves, and Proverbs may well present the thoughts of an older person.[1] Through this chapter, then, I hope to answer the question: What does biblical wisdom have to say about old age? And we wonder how we should adopt the perspectives presented in order to reorient our approach to life if necessary.

JOB AND FRIENDS DEFICIENT IN WISDOM?

The bulk of the book of Job record the dispute between Job and his three friends; all are old. Each man offers his understanding on God and life under his rule, and they do not mince words in telling what they think about each other. The dispute pits two opposing factions, Job in one corner and

---

1. Crenshaw includes the non-canonical writings of the book of Sirach or Ecclesiasticus and the Wisdom of Solomon as the fuller wisdom corpus within Jewish literature (*Old Testament Wisdom*). He also covers the wisdom from ancient Egypt and Mesopotamia.

his three friends in the other. The conflict between them centers on Job's alleged guilt in view of his suffering. Their age is not central until Elihu speaks (Job 32–37). When the four men stop speaking, he finally interjects after remaining silent throughout their debate because they are older than he (Job 32:4). Indeed, he states the matter explicitly (Job 32:6b–9). *Elihu cites a general understanding to which Asian cultures generally adhere and practice—the repository of wisdom lies in the aged who have accumulated knowledge and understanding over the years. Elihu, like Asian young people, defers to the old men.* Patiently he waits until they finish, although disappointed with Job for his self-justification at God's expense and with his friends for failing to refute him (Job 32:2–3). Elihu then subtly criticizes them by observing that age alone does not guarantee wisdom. The source of true wisdom is "the spirit in a person, the breath of the Almighty." Hence, Elihu also adds that he too possesses wisdom and understanding.

Although culture conditions the young to expect wisdom from the elderly, the old must still confirm the assumption by displaying that virtue. If they do not, they may lose the respect of the young. Later, Job regains children to replace those who died and doubles his possessions (Job 42:10–15). We infer he regains the respect of all who know him (Job 42:11). But this reversal comes from God.

PROVERBS OF SOLOMON

This collection of proverbs credits Solomon, Agur (Prov 30:1–33), and King Lemuel (Prov 31:1–31) explicitly, and the writer(s) of the thirty sayings of the wise (Prov 22:17—24:22) and further sayings of the wise (Prov 24:23–34) remain anonymous, although Solomon or someone else may have collected these sayings for inclusion.[2]

The primary allusion to ageism in Proverbs comes in the form of a father's admonition to his son.[3] The older person giving instruction may be a biological father or someone who fulfills the role as a father figure, mentor, teacher, counselor, or guide. If the son or younger person accepts the instruction, they are labeled wise, otherwise fools. The sharp dichotomy, typical of Proverbs, leaves no middle ground. The only scenario presented

---

2. Waltke, *Proverbs, Chapters 1–15*, 24.

3. Prov 1:8–19; 2:1—7:27; 10:1; 13:1; 15:5, 20; 23:15–28; 24:13–14; 27:11; 28:7; 31:1–9.

depicts a diligent father, earnest in his instruction; but the scene can vary depending on the teachability of the son.

WISDOM OF QOHELET

Ecclesiastes preserves the musing of the Teacher after considerable effort to craft his thoughts in order to present what is upright and true (Eccl 12:9–10). His accomplishments, observations, and thoughts suggest that he may be near the end of his life, now an old man.

Qohelet's Observations

Interpreters have wrestled with the meaning of Eccl 12:1–6, many opting to regard it as an allegory about old age.[4] Before looking at this passage, however, we review Qohelet's comments about youth that precede immediately before, thinking perhaps the writer intends to contrast the young and old, as he has facilitated contrast elsewhere.[5] He begins with the declaration that the sun's light enables people to see the sun and all that the world contains (Eccl 11:7). Earlier, he wrote, "Then I saw that wisdom surpasses foolishness as light surpasses darkness" (Eccl 2:13). In both incidences, the writer utilizes the physical properties of light in normal life situations to depict the obvious preference for and advantages of light over darkness.

Given that Eccl 11:9–10 clearly addresses the young, we infer that Eccl 11:8 applies to the young as well and states two admonitions: (1) enjoy all the years of your life, however many you will have, and (2) expect many days of darkness as characterizing life. Any given day can be light or dark. Earlier, Qohelet writes something similar (Eccl 7:14): "On the day of prosperity be happy, but on the day of adversity consider: God has made the

---

4. For example, Crenshaw interprets Eccl 12:1–8 as "the debilitating effects of inevitable decay" (*Old Testament Wisdom*, 131) and Alter more forthrightly states "the personal catastrophe of aging" (*Wisdom Books*, 387–89). See also Wright, "Ecclesiastes," 5:1191–94; Longman, *Ecclesiastes*, 262–72; and Seow, *Ecclesiastes*, 352. However, Longman and Seow hesitate regarding the entire section as allegorical, noting that some of the metaphors may not allude to old age or should be taken literally as referring to something else.

5. The wise vs. the fool, Eccl 2:13–14, although both share the same fate, Eccl 2:15–16; the one pleasing God vs. the sinner, Eccl 2:26 and 8:12–13, although injustice prevails, Eccl 8:14; the living vs. the dead, Eccl 9:4–5, but the living cannot escape eventual death, Eccl 9:3; God vs. humanity, Eccl 3:9–14, 5:2, and 8:17.

one as well as the other so that a person will not discover anything that will come after him." Good and bad days do not necessarily correlate with a person's wisdom or foolishness, or with their moral condition. The warning that there will be many dark days prepares the young to expect them. Then Eccl 11:8e concludes with "everything that is to come will be futility." The idea seems to be unpredictability or uncertainty and things not making sense. Carrying the metaphor and its implication a bit further, we might say that, if light is sweet, then darkness must be bitter. Possible connotations come to mind—unpleasant thoughts and emotions, perhaps grief, remorse and regret, painful or anxiety-inducing experiences.

Qohelet urges the young to be joyful and to pursue their heart's desire (Eccl 11:9abc). But he warns them to remember that God will hold them accountable for the decisions they make and the path they take (Eccl 11:9d). In the next verse (Eccl 11:10), the directive to cast off anxiety or unpleasantness from the heart and troubles or pain from the body suggests that youth possess an ability that the old lack. The old, unlike the young, may not have many years left, a fact that resides in the forefront of their thoughts.

However, Qohelet does not provide a clear demarcation between the young and the old—when does a person transition from youth to old age? But one constant characterizes both: many "days of darkness," suggesting that life, regardless of a person's stage in life, is challenging, difficult, disappointing at times, maybe even painful. The overall perspective of Ecclesiastes supports that understanding. In that regard, do the young have an advantage over the old? Yes, as Eccl 11:10a informs us: the young can "remove sorrow from your heart and keep pain away from your body," something the old cannot easily do.

Qohelet's One Positive Advice: Carpe Diem

In the overall context of Ecclesiastes, carpe diem represents the one clear positive by which Qohelet exhorts readers to find satisfaction and joy (Eccl 2:24–25; 3:12–13, 22; 5:18–19; 8:15; 9:7–9). Indeed, each carpe diem admonition follows a negative statement about life—Eccl 2:24–25 follows the lament about leaving the fruit of one's labor to a successor (Eccl 2:17–23); Eccl 3:12–13 follows the admission of humanity's inability to discern the proper time for each and every activity nor to discern God's activities (Eccl 3:1–11); Eccl 3:22 follows the sobering realization that humanity has no advantage over the animals with regard to death (Eccl 3:18–21); Eccl 5:18–19 follows the "sickening evil" that no one can take whatever profit achieved in life with them after death (Eccl 5:15–16) and the characterization of life as darkness punctuated with frustration, affliction, and anger (Eccl 5:17); Eccl 8:15 follows the observation of foulness or injustice when the righteous and wicked do not receive the consequences appropriate to their moral profile (Eccl 8:14); and Eccl 9:7–9 follows the somber and hopeless state of the dead (Eccl 9:2–6). In view of this repeated allusion to carpe diem, then, the exhortation to rejoice (Eccl 11:8) connotes embracing the momentary joys and pleasures of life. This is the best that humanity can hope to attain in life.

The pattern of citing some negative or evil in life followed immediately with an exhortation to carpe diem signifies Qohelet's advice on how readers should respond to the difficulties, incongruities, and disappointments they will encounter. Rather than dwell on negative thoughts and feelings, they should pursue carpe diem as the only thing within their control provided God permits (Eccl 2:24b–26). Practicing this advice lessens the sting and sense of hopelessness that threaten to overwhelm. However, it is only temporary relief and requires constant implementation. In a sense, this practice seems like survival mode.

Hebel, a critical motif in Ecclesiastes, occurring thirty-eight times there compared to seventy-three times elsewhere in the OT,[6] conveys three nuances—insubstantiality, transience, and, foulness.[7] Insubstantiality refers to something that appears promising but fails to deliver resulting in deep disappointment. Transience alludes to the brevity of life. And foulness speaks of injustice and even perversion. Hope in one's work morphs into disappointment when what appears substantial fails to meet expectations—insubstantiality. The inevitability of death looms heavily when one looks into the future—transience; this realization deeply troubles the writer. And life can be unfair where justice is elusive or subverted—foulness. *Hebel* impacts young and old without discrimination. With more life experience, do the old handle the implications of *hebel* better than the young?

---

6. Seow, *Ecclesiastes*, 101.

7. Miller, *Symbol and Rhetoric in Ecclesiastes*, 152.

Qohelet, a Biblical Exception?

Qohelet's advice labeled carpe diem seems to run counter to what Scripture in general directs. For example, Prov 3:5–12 states:

> Trust in the Lord with all your heart and do not lean on your own understanding. In all your ways acknowledge him, and he will make your paths straight. Do not be wise in your own eyes; fear the Lord and turn away from evil. It will be healing to your body and refreshment to your bones. Honor the Lord from your wealth, and from the first of all your produce; then your barns will be filled with plenty, and your vats will overflow with new wine. My son, do not reject the discipline of the Lord or loathe his rebuke, for whom the Lord loves he disciplines, just as a father disciplines the son in whom he delights.

The writer of Proverbs depicts a loving relationship between a person and God who functions as a father. God delights in and loves his child. The implied intimacy invites complete trust in the Lord even when things defy one's ability to understand and to pursue a course of action that provides some assurance of success. Clearly the child of God steers a life course that avoids evil and pursues righteousness, honoring the Lord in specific ways. The promises inherent in this passage assure of the Lord's intervention to make straight paths.

Then our subject passage exhorts readers: "do not reject the discipline of the Lord or loathe his rebuke" (Prov 3:11). This admonition positions us to expect the Lord's discipline that confronts and corrects unwanted patterns of behavior. The child of God ought to fully accept the discipline meted out although unpleasant and even painful. Discipline showcases the Father's love and legitimizes the relationship with his child.

As we review this one sample as representative of the general teaching of Scripture and the proper attitude toward and the interaction with the divine, we discover an apparent discrepancy with what we find in Ecclesiastes. In general, Scripture depicts the relationship between God and his subjects as family, Father and child. The Father desires his child to conform to a life of righteousness and reinforces his will through loving discipline. But even a survey of Qohelet's writings fails to confirm any functional relationship between God and the writer and, by implication, between God and the reader. Any direct relationship consisting of personal interaction going both ways appears very muted at best.

Aside from these admonitions, the writer seems content to simply record his observations about God and reality in a matter-of-fact manner. For example, he laments (Eccl 2:17), "So I hated life, for the work which had been done under the sun was unhappy to me; because everything is futility and striving after wind." "Futility" refers to transience in view of the immediately preceding observation that the wise has no advantage over the fool in regard to the inevitability of death (Eccl 2:14b–16). The writer makes no appeal to God either for a longer life or for some assurance that being wise really holds a significant advantage over the fool. Again, he states (Eccl 3:10–11): "I have seen the task which God has given the sons of mankind with which to occupy themselves. He has made everything appropriate in its time. He has also set eternity in their heart, without the possibility that mankind will find out the work which God has done from the beginning even to the end." In context, the burden refers to the proper timing for every event (Eccl 3:1–8) for which God holds humanity responsible. But humans cannot comprehend his activities and desired timing (Eccl 3:11). Curiously, the writer does not urge his readers to seek God's guidance and will through prayer. He plaintively states a fact that humans can do nothing about. Then, from another text, we read (Eccl 6:1–2): "There is an evil which I have seen under the sun, and it is widespread among mankind: a person to whom God has given riches, wealth, and honor, so that his soul lacks nothing of all that he desires, yet God has not given him the opportunity to enjoy these things, but a foreigner enjoys them. This is futility and a severe affliction." The potential benefits of acquiring wealth and honor are thwarted when God prevents the accompanying enjoyment. No prayer to God to rectify the situation emerges. At most, the writer simply complains about the injustice as if to indicate that nothing can be resolved. A third example (Eccl 8:17—9:1) declares:

> I saw every work of God, I concluded that one cannot discover the work which has been done under the sun. Even though a person laboriously seeks, he will not discover; and even if the wise person claims to know, he cannot discover. For I have taken all this to my heart, even to examine it all, that righteous people, wise people, and their deeds are in the hand of God. People do not know whether it will be love or hatred; anything awaits them.

Here Qohelet can discern God's handiwork but cannot fully comprehend much about it. Human wisdom has limitations, something that Qohelet may have attempted to overcome without success. Again, we find no effort to ask God to reveal his secrets or to praise him for his inscrutability. He seems to view or study God rather passively as an object of his observations and investigation. He makes no attempt to interact with God. We look in vain for any evidence of a personal relationship. Even the prophetic literature, in spite of the predominant negative tone where God rebukes and warns his people, provides a greater glimpse of the relationship. Ecclesiastes omits any direct allusion to a covenant between God and his people that so typifies the rest of Scripture, but aligns well with Proverbs where the covenant fades into the background and practical observations and admonitions come to the foreground. Yet, both Ecclesiastes and Proverbs highlight fearing God (Eccl 3:14; 5:7; 8:12–13; 12:13; and Prov 1:7, 29; 2:5; 3:7; 8:13; 9:10; 10:27; 14:2, 16, 26–27; 15:16, 33; 16:6; 19:23; 22:4; 23:17; 24:21; 31:30).

Hence, there seems to be an unbridgeable divide between God and humanity, the most noble representative being the wise who, like Qohelet, views the Lord as remote and transcendent. With regard to old age, then, Ecclesiastes does not encourage the reader to approach God about the matter, either for advice or assurance of any kind. This lack leaves two questions in the mind of the reader unanswered: (1) Does God care that we may experience apprehension about the issues associated with this latter phase in life? (2) Is he able to alleviate our anxiety and struggles caused by old age?

Symptoms of Advanced Age or Not?

After writing about and addressing the young (Eccl 11:7–10), Qohelet follows with (Eccl 12:1): "Remember also your Creator in the days of your youth, before the evil days come and the years approach when you will say, 'I have no pleasure in them.'" The reference to a later period in which they will find no pleasure echoes Barzillai's sentiments (2 Sam 19:35), connoting old age. Then follows a lengthy and poetic description (Eccl 12:2–5abcd),[8] including the darkened celestial lights, clouds after the rain, a puzzling description of almond trees blossoming and grasshoppers, followed by the explicit mention of death ("man goes to his eternal home while the mourners

---

8. Seow reviews the debate among scholars about the interpretation of Eccl 12:2–5, whether to read it allegorically, literally, or figuratively (*Ecclesiastes*, 372–74). He seems to favor a mix of the literal and figurative. Based on the syntax, Fox interprets Eccl 12:2–5 as a depiction of death and mourning rather than the aging process (*Qohelet and His Contradictions*, 286–89).

move around in the street," Eccl 12:5e). As one scholar proposes, this section recalls the prophets describing the disaster that overtakes the people on a nationwide scale in symbolic language.[9] Qohelet, however, confines such language to the individual. Given the universal scope of the symbolism, it appears that the inevitable scenario of death encompasses all humanity. Another scholar posits that the intervening verses (Eccl 12:2–5abcd) contrast the transience of humanity and the permanence of nature.[10] Rejecting the common view that the text contains an allegory about old age, the scholar finds instead the figure of a house in ruins (Eccl 12:3–5abcd) representing humanity's downfall.[11] This thought surfaces repeatedly in Qohelet's exasperated writings (Eccl 1:3; 2:11, 17–23; 3:9–11, 18–20; 4:1–4; 5:8–17; 6:1–12; 8:9–14; 9:1–3, 11–12). What this scholar labels as nature is what Qohelet laments as events under the sun that lie outside of human control. Then from birth to death passing through the years of youth and the period of old age, life remains one constant struggle with *hebel*—insubstantiality, transience, and foulness.

Preoccupation with Death

Qohelet has already shown a preoccupation with death throughout his musings. Despite his incomparable wisdom and great success with a number of noteworthy enterprises (Eccl 1:16; 2:4–10), he laments the limitations of wisdom and the transience of his satisfaction with his achievements because of the inevitability of death (Eccl 2:14b–23). His wisdom does not exempt him from the fate of the fool—death. And with that end in view, he grieves about giving up the fruit of all his labor to a successor, particularly if that person proves unworthy. But even if the successor is honorable, Qohelet still hates his inability to keep anything (Eccl 2:17–18). Hate is a very strong term. He directs his hatred toward life because his life's work is grievous or evil (Eccl 2:17) and even toward his own labor because someone else will benefit from it (Eccl 2:18). Here, I believe, Qohelet complains that life is not fair. Twice *hebel* appears in this section (Eccl 2:17 and 2:23).

---

9. Fox, *Qohelet and His Contradictions*, 290–94. Fox samples such cataclysmic descriptions from Jer 25:10–11a; Ezek 32:7–8; Joel 2:2a, 6, 10b; Isa 13:9b–10. He cites other passages as well. These depict divine judgment against a guilty people.

10. Sawyer, "Ruined House in Ecclesiastes 12," 519–31.

11. Sawyer, "Ruined House in Ecclesiastes 12," 524–29.

The first occurrence refers to transience and the second to foulness and insubstantiality.

The specter of death resurfaces in Eccl 3:18–22 where Qohelet states that both humans and animals share the same fate—death. Earlier he depicts the same leveling of the wise and the fool in that the former, in spite of possessing wisdom, cannot avoid death (Eccl 2:14–16). Later (Eccl 9:1–6), another leveling exists between the righteous and the wicked, the good and the bad, and the clean and the unclean in that all, regardless of moral profile, face death. Then a passing comment arises in Eccl 5:15–17 that laments nothing gained in life can be kept at death, calling it a "sickening evil" and toiling "for the wind." Additional brief allusions appear in Eccl 6:3c, 6:6c, 7:1, 7:17, 8:8b, 8:10, and 9:10. Then comes the description of life as "the few years of his futile life; he will spend them like a shadow" (Eccl 6:12), emphasizing the brevity of life with an overpowering sense of the temporary. Here "futile" likely connotes transience.

The repeated references to death suggest that Qohelet may be in his twilight years, to which we older people readily relate. Inadvertently, we older folks may be counting down our remaining days and, as some have shared with me, waiting to die. Rather morbid but understandable to some degree. With his incessant preoccupation with death, more specifically his own demise, Qohelet darkens his writings, making it rather somber reading. Although his statements are general, addressed to all humanity about their mortality, yet he seems more concerned about his own death. Thus, Ecclesiastes comes across as an extended soliloquy. We get the impression that the writer harbors no hope, no recourse to alleviate his darken mood. If we adopt his point of view, we would become depressed—life is not only too short, it is also insubstantial and foul. We too would quote him in declaring (Eccl 12:8), "'Futility of futilities,' says the Preacher, 'all is futility!'"[12]

However, we need to see our remaining time, even if very little, as God's gift and mandate. What does he want us to do until he calls us home? Instead of being fixated on our impending demise, let us cultivate a sense of urgency to redeem the fast-dwindling available time. Citing a modern colloquialism, we say, "Make it count."

---

12. Seow identifies two ways the superlative can be expressed, one of which is the construct chain as used in Eccl 12:8 (*Grammar*, 76). Thus, "futility of futilities" denotes the most futile or the greatest futility.

Partial Response to Qohelet

Unlike Qohelet, I suggest that we don't get overly concerned about our successors, whether worthy or not. First, we may have no influence on who follows after us. Second, when they take over, we may not be around to see how they fare. Third, each person is accountable for how well they live and work. Our responsibility is limited to what we hand over to the next person. Then that person must answer for how they fulfill their stewardship.

As humans we are fully aware of our mortality. A couple of modern proverbs have circulated confirming this reality, one famously declaring, "the only certainties in life are death and taxes," and the other opining, "the only certainty life contains is death."[13] So do we need to afflict ourselves with unnecessary angst and foreboding? Must we fixate on death? Indeed, worry will not lengthen our lives, as Jesus proclaims (Matt 6:27). If anything, worry may shorten our lives because stress or inner tension adversely affects our emotional and mental well-being. Instead of being plagued by worry (Matt 6:25–32, 34), Jesus admonishes his disciples to focus on his kingdom and righteousness (Matt 6:33), trusting in the heavenly Father's provision (Matt 6:32b).

A closer reading of Ecclesiastes uncovers two major deficiencies in Qohelet's approach to life. Sometimes what is not stated can be as important, even more so, than what is stated. First, as I noted earlier, Qohelet does not enjoy any kind of discernable relationship with God. Except for his dispassionate advice about having a listening posture when entering the house of God (Eccl 5:1–3) and fulfilling one's vows to God (Eccl 5:4–7), he never documents any prayer or even a lament to God. There is no attempt at direct communication. God is cloaked in mystery as Qohelet states (Eccl 3:11b): "He has also set eternity in their heart, without the possibility that mankind will find out the work which God has done from the beginning even to the end." No human, including Qohelet, can penetrate the mystery of God's work. Then he adds (Eccl 8:16–17): "When I devoted my mind to know wisdom and to see the business which has been done on the earth (even though one should never sleep day or night), and I saw every work of God, I concluded that one cannot discover the work which has been done under the sun. Even though a person laboriously seeks, he will not discover; and even if the wise person claims to know, he cannot discover."

---

13. The first proverb comes from American writer Mark Twain, who may have quoted Benjamin Franklin, and the second originates with writer Patricia Briggs.

Qohelet bemoans that his vast wisdom proves insufficient to comprehend God's inner workings, plans, purpose, and rationale. He views God from afar, that God is in heaven and he is confined to earth (Eccl 5:2b). The oft repeated motif "under the sun"[14] and equivalent "under heaven" (Eccl 1:13; 2:3; 3:1) reinforce Qohelet's limited worldview, bounded by this life and events in this world. God operates above in heaven, not under the sun. Hence, God and his work lie beyond Qohelet's observation. The distance between God and our writer is unbridgeable.

Second, Qohelet appears isolated without any meaningful human contact. He does not participate in any community.[15] Hence, he does not consult with anyone else about his observations, insights, and thoughts, implying that he does not seek confirmation of his point of view nor does he desire a sounding board. He lacks any kind of support network, no allies or friends. His isolation likely exacerbates his sense of gloom and darkness. Ecclesiastes represents Qohelet's rumination, negative thoughts repeatedly come to the forefront, so much so that his anxiety and distress deepen. Even his one positive advice, carpe diem, will lessen in benefit.

Hence, these two deficiencies, distance from God and the lack of a supporting community, can hasten Qohelet's demise. If these two factors characterize us, we lead a woeful existence compounded by the normal ravages of old age. Then the solution seems obvious—close the distance from God through prayer and other spiritual disciplines, confessing any moral failings, and seek to join a community that provides support. If we have been delinquent in either area for a protracted length of time, we face two hurdles, however. One, inertia: we do not practice the habit of relating to God. Good habits take time and effort to cultivate. Two, finding the right community may not be easy. What if such a community is not readily available locally? How do we go about finding such a group? What traits should characterize the group? The answers may not be so easy to acquire.

Looking Back at Our Past

It is one thing to pine for the youth years, wishing to relive them and ignoring the present; it is another matter to review the earlier years in order to

---

14. Eccl 1:3, 9, 14; 2:17–20, 22; 3:16; 4:1, 3, 7, 15; 5:13, 18; 6:1, 12; 8:9, 15 (2x), 17; 9:3, 6, 9 (2x), 11, 13; 10:5.

15. Fox makes this observation (*Qohelet and His Contradictions*, 294).

evaluate and to learn. The youth years can serve as a foundation for subsequent years. Lived well, they can secure the older years.

Qohelet: Lived Well?

Did Qohelet live well? When he looks back over his life and pursuits, he becomes disillusioned and seemingly depressed. His conclusion shocks and disturbs us, declaring (Eccl 1:2): "'Futility of futilities,' says the Preacher, 'Futility of futilities! All is futility.'" In the overall context of Ecclesiastes, he means that all is transient, insubstantial, and foul. In effect, he cannot find significance or lasting value in anything he has accomplished or strived for as he locates his career and life within the overall scheme of things (Eccl 1:3—2:11). He summarizes his frustration thus: "What is crooked cannot be straightened, and what is lacking cannot be counted" (Eccl 1:15). This statement finds an echo in his rhetorical question (Eccl 7:13): "Consider the work of God, for who is able to straighten what he has bent?" Here "bent" and "straighten" do not bear a moral nuance but rather reflect a metaphorical contrastive pair depicting certain realities. Conditions or events may exist or happen in one manner or in a different manner. That's life. A related statement appears at Eccl 3:14: "I know that everything God does will remain forever; there is nothing to add to it and there is nothing to take from it. And God has so worked, that people will fear him." Qohelet understands human limitations—some things lie outside human control and influence. This reality points to God's sovereign authority as evident in the various situations in life. They remind us that we are but human and much less than God in capability, accomplishment, and exercise of the will. But Qohelet cannot accept this truth, it seems. Or rather, his ambition will not permit him to accept it. His grand enterprises reveal his driving ambition (Eccl 2:4–10). But as he reviews his achievements, however monumental, he sees the vast gulf separating him from God. He cannot participate in God's grand enterprises. This realization ought to generate fear toward God, and it does; but his ambition seeks a fuller partnership with God. He thinks true significance lies there. Anything less than that lofty position is unacceptable. His standards for living well exceed human capability. Even though he knows his place, he struggles with his limitations.

The Frame Narrator: Living Well

The frame narrator[16] provides an important corrective for Qohelet's viewpoint, without which, we too may experience Qohelet's angst. With the last two verses of Ecclesiastes as our guide, we can navigate toward a more satisfying life through a more realistic sense of self, if we live and work within our boundaries and have a healthier relationship with our Lord. We may evaluate our lives as well lived if we fear the Lord and keep his commandments faithfully. We know our place and gladly accept it. We remember Qohelet's words: "For God is in heaven and you are on the earth" (Eccl 5:2b). This is the basis by which God will judge us in the end.

In actuality, God alone will determine whether we have lived well or not (Eccl 12:14). But we can still perform periodic reality checks as we live out our lives, pursuing our dreams and goals and fulfilling our various responsibilities. With the Scriptures as our benchmark, especially the Wisdom literature, we have guidance and criteria to evaluate ourselves, to make mid-course corrections if needed or to affirm proper attitude and conduct. And the frame narrator keeps things very simple, although not easy to observe. Do this faithfully and we may have the confidence of having lived well.

Did We Live Well in Our Past?

Based on the frame narrator's criteria, we may assess that Qohelet lives well. But obviously he does not agree. By any usual standard, we believe he leads an amazing life and achieves some awe-inspiring milestones. Yet, he experiences major disappointment and disillusionment to the extent he views life, at least his, as meaningless or absurd. However, he still offers valuable insights as the frame narrator also acknowledges. Hence, we should read both writers in combination, using the framer narrator as the lens to interpret

---

16. Some commentators discern a frame narrator distinct from Qohelet, the main author of Ecclesiastes. See, for example, Fox who identifies several distinct persona or voices—Qohelet, the frame-narrator, and possibly someone else who writes the epilogue to provide a more traditional stance (*Time to Tear Down*, 363–75). Ecclesiastes features an opening frame, 1:1–11, and the epilogue, 12:9–14. Also, Longman, *Ecclesiastes*, 274. Payne identifies three voices—the voice of the transmitter who functions as buffer between the orthodox view of the rest of Scripture and Qohelet's more radical view, Qohelet himself, and finally the voice of Piety ("Voices of Ecclesiastes," 286–90). In general agreement, Wilson prefers to label the narrator as the epilogist(s), influenced by Proverbs 1–9 ("'Words of the Wise,'" 189).

Qohelet. In this manner, we would be better positioned to evaluate how well we lived in our past as we look back over the years.

But what would be our motivation to do so? We may think that our past is unalterable and, although we may have some regrets, we cannot do anything about it. Long habitual behavioral patterns are nearly impossible to be replaced with new habits. We are too old to change. Moreover, in old age we think we do not have much of a runway left to make a significant difference. Can a long life misspent be meaningfully rectified by doing the right thing in what little time we have left?

Scriptural analogy and examples motivate us to do the right thing even up to the final moment of life. First, the frame narrator declares, "for God will bring every act to judgment, everything which is hidden, whether it is good or evil" (Eccl 12:14)—"every act" encompasses every spoken word, thought, or action throughout one's life from youth through to and including old age until the moment of death. We continue to be accountable to God in our twilight years. Neither Scripture in general nor Ecclesiastes in particular hint that God's criteria or standard of evaluation changes when we enter our final years. Second, God urges Ezekiel to call the people to repentance (Ezek 33:10–20), warning that righteous deeds done before will not cover present evil but exhorting the wicked to turn from sin to do right so that their former wickedness will be forgotten. Thus, even if our earlier years are marked by failure morally or otherwise, our later years can potentially supersede the former period. Third, Scripture portrays Jesus and Paul finishing well. Knowing that his crucifixion is nearly finished, Jesus intentionally fulfills prophecy by announcing his thirst (John 19:28–30). He wants every aspect of this event completed to the last detail in accordance to the divine will. Likewise, Paul expresses his determination to finish his race and to complete his mission even if he would encounter affliction and imprisonment (Acts 20:22–24). Later, he affirms that he has fought the good fight, finished the race, and kept the faith, thereby justifiably anticipating the crown of righteousness (2 Tim 4:6–8). Like Paul, we too can look forward to our reward from our Lord, the righteous judge (2 Tim 4:8), if we finish well.

But our past may have created barriers making it more difficult to finish well. What we must realize is that our past has molded us to become who we are today.[17] Taking a hard, objective review of past relationships and events that created the script for why we react and behave the way we

---

17. See, for example, Scazzero's readable *Emotionally Healthy Spirituality*, 93–115.

do can generate greater self-awareness. Armed with this self-understanding and submitting ourselves to the indwelling Spirit's authority and power, we can turn things around to lead a God-honoring life in our final years.

Assessing Our Life Overall

To label our life as a success or failure seems extreme. Is it really a hit or miss proposition? Woe to those who evaluate themselves as a failure. Does that imply a totally wasted life? Or what if we think our life is a success? Will that inflate our ego? What do we mean by success or failure anyway? What criteria ought we use? Should we even try to make such an assessment?

Qohelet's obsession with death whereby he regards all his accomplishments as a source of deep disappointment, because death hampers all attempts at longevity, prompts us to examine his criterion carefully. We agree that death is an inevitable fate for all. As a common fate shared by humans and beasts and by the wise and the fool, Qohelet laments any real advantage that humans have over animals or the wise over fools. However, we wonder whether he prizes quantity over quality. He minimizes the magnificence of his achievements made possible by his unparalleled wisdom and personal resources. His is the ultimate human endeavor unmatched by anyone else. Yet, his inevitable death robs him of any lasting satisfaction, temporarily gratified but not permanently. His sense of failure is overwhelming. A major clue to his dissatisfaction focuses on having to leave the fruits of his labor to someone else who has not toiled as he has (Eccl 2:18–23). This realization causes him anxiety, grief, restlessness especially at night. We have already pointed out this dilemma of his previously.

We might agree with Qohelet if we care only about our own benefits. He appears very self-absorbed, only concerned about his own well-being. He omits any mention of possible benefits to anyone else from all his lofty pursuits. Yet, parents do not usually think this way; they want to pass some heritage and inheritance on to their children. And those of us ministering to the next generation want to bless them and prepare them for life through our labor. Many of us serve sacrificially, not thinking about any kind of compensation for ourselves. Hopefully, we leave some imprint in their lives that carries on after our time concludes. In a sense, we live on through the young people in what influence we exert. This effort represents our investment in the future, not our own but that of others. Qohelet displays no desire to invest in anyone else. Then we can understand his disappointment.

In Asian cultures, for example, the Filipino and Malay, families deeply respect their grandparents, viewing them as the source of wisdom and seeking their advice and guidance. For the religious Malays, Islam reinforces the children's devotion to the older generation through schools and prayers. Their duty to the elderly is religious in nature. The bonds across the generations are very strong. The older generation find great satisfaction investing in young people's lives. For Filipinos, the bonds are more cultural than religious but no less close. Interestingly in Thailand, the Thai Chinese have a much tighter bond between the generations compared to the Thai Thais. In the latter group, the older people, being essentially hands-off, give the young considerable freedom to make their own decisions. The Asian elderly do not, as a rule, suffer Qohelet's anxiety about those who inherit the fruits of his labor. Even if the children may exhibit questionable character, the grandparents teach them moral principles and challenge them to lead useful lives.

This observation about Qohelet and his criterion for success provides the impetus to redefine what we should consider success versus failure. He sees himself as a failure, and we agree but for a different reason. His death limits the heights and victories he can aspire to achieve for personal glory and enjoyment. Because of his wisdom, unparalleled wealth, and amazing opportunities, Qohelet represents the pinnacle of human ability and accomplishment. He attains every worldly (under the sun) success, exceeding the dreams of all others. In contrast, we see our finite life span as a major motivation to extend our lives through investing in the next generation, who will benefit from our legacy and, in a way, carry on the banner we raise in life. Qohelet fails to invest in others until he becomes the Teacher (Eccl 12:9–10). If we make the same mistake, then we too will experience disappointment, anxiety, and distress. We will regard death as the great barrier limiting our success.

Another difference between Qohelet and us can be the participation in a community, a term that connotes family, guild, social group, and alliance of like-minded people (such as a special interest group or faith community). Strikingly, Qohelet appears alone and isolated, a distant observer of humanity and even of God. The prominent trait is distance devoid of any meaningful interaction or mutual interdependence. He is isolated; whether he feels loneliness is unknown. He seeks no advice, instruction, guidance, or encouragement from anyone, and enjoys no affiliation with anyone. Does anyone teach him at an early point of his life? Do the various references to being taught or having a teacher in Proverbs apply to him?[18] Moreover, his musings show no prayer life. He seems content in his self-sufficiency, not realizing that that apparent strength can also be his weakness. We all need to belong to a community (for example Heb 10:24–25). David has his advisors; Jesus regularly interacts with the Father in prayer; Paul has his team-oriented ministry and traveling companions. The Psalter, for example, alludes to the assembly of the righteous where they gather for worship and fellowship (Pss 1:5; 7:7; 22:22, 25; 111:1).[19] And we all need God, even Qohelet.

Living Our Present

The one prevailing advice Qohelet repeatedly gives concerns the principle of carpe diem, making the most of the present moment, the here-and-now. The focus is not so narrow, however, to imply only this instant but rather a relatively brief time frame that can encompass the hour, day, week, or whatever period inferring the present time. Qohelet does not mark off a precise time duration. He advises readers to enjoy the present activity where eating and drinking and toil constitute a synecdoche for any and all activity typifying ordinary life, nothing special or unique. They should find satisfaction in their toil or labor. Satisfaction may connote successful pursuit and completion of some task or activity, doing something worthwhile, at least, to the worker. It may also infer receiving some desired or expected compensation that corresponds to the effort made. Qohelet's non-specificity invites a number of possible interpretations where, it seems, all may be viable—meals with family and friends, pleasurable pastimes, home responsibilities, personal projects, helping a neighbor, church-related activities, marketplace duties, and the like. He makes no differentiation or prioritization. All such activities fit within the overarching umbrella of carpe diem. Immediate gratification is emphasized, although that would not preclude long-term plans and objectives as Qohelet himself demonstrates (Eccl 2:4–10) where he takes delight in all his labor, which is his reward (Eccl 2:10). Some of the enterprises undertaken represent significant investment in planning, mobilizing resources, and execution that likely require years to complete. All these activities still illustrate carpe diem, living in the present.

---

18. Prov 1:8; 3:1; 4:2; 5:13; 6:20; 7:2; 9:9.
19. A few references (Pss 82:1; 89:5) may allude to the heavenly host.

The chief characteristic of carpe diem is that all such activities and associated benefits are temporary. Qohelet bemoans this fact when he laments: "So I considered all my activities which my hands had done and the labor which I had exerted, and behold, all was futility and striving after wind, and there was no benefit under the sun" (Eccl 2:11). His earlier assessment about life "under the sun" (Eccl 1:2–11) where he complains that "there is nothing new under the sun" (Eccl 1:9b) and that each generation is quickly forgotten by the next (Eccl 1:11) provides the context for his declaration in Eccl 2:11. His verdict that everything is meaningless or absurd (*hebel*) connotes transience and insubstantiality. His great hopes and ambition in undertaking his various projects (Eccl 2:3c–4a) meet with equally great disappointment and disillusionment (Eccl 2:11). His accomplishments will soon be forgotten in not leaving a permanent mark and not making a significant change in the grand scheme of things.

Here we must disagree with Qohelet. If we invest in the next generation as discussed earlier, will we not make a permanent mark that endures beyond our own lives and will not our successors remember us with gratitude for having impacted their lives? But even if they should forget us, their lives will bear the imprint of our ministry to them. *Asian grandparents and parents would agree. The children and grandchildren take top priority. And the young people are grateful.*

Thus, carpe diem confines itself to enjoying the moment and finding limited satisfaction, not being concerned about the big picture or about anything of lasting value—severely myopic. But this orientation prevents suffering disappointment or disillusionment with life. This viewpoint also accepts human finiteness and limitations. It acknowledges the vast gulf separating humanity from God, who alone achieves permanence in all that he does without outside contribution from anyone else, especially humans (Eccl 3:14). This truth we freely and gladly acknowledge in contrast to what we discern to be Qohelet's begrudging recognition.

Moreover, the practice of carpe diem represents acceptance of and conformance to God's will. Qohelet confirms that fact (Eccl 5:19–20): "Furthermore, as for every person to whom God has given riches and wealth, he has also given him the opportunity to enjoy them and to receive his reward and rejoice in his labor; this is the gift of God. For he will not often call to mind the years of his life, because God keeps him busy with the joy of his heart." Unless God grants the ability to enjoy life, people will not experience joy and happiness regardless of how well-situated they may be. Thus, carpe diem is God's gift, expressing his will. Hence, living by faith and dependence on the Lord positions a person to discern the gift and to express gratitude to him. This outlook aligns with Jesus' admonition to abstain from worry about the necessities of life (Matt 6:25–32). But Qohelet stops short of Jesus' charge: "But seek first his kingdom and his righteousness, and all these things will be provided to you" (Matt 6:33).[20] The frame narrator, however, covers Jesus' charge with one of his own, "fear God and keep his commandments, because this applies to every person" (Eccl 12:13b). The frame narrator infers the definition of righteousness. Here then is an example where the frame narrator's interjection fills out a deficiency in Qohelet's musing in order to bring the point of view of the whole book to conform to scriptural teaching elsewhere.

There is an interesting note that Qohelet adds when he observes that God purposefully occupies humanity with gladness and joy. Preoccupied with the enjoyment of life and work, humans rarely think about life in broader strokes. In this regard, Qohelet proves to be the exception as he does ponder the bigger picture. Based on his negative reaction throughout his writings concluding that everything is meaningless or absurd, however, we surmise the reason behind God occupying us with momentary pleasure. Perhaps God wants to protect our fragile psyche and sense of self-importance. Could we be happy about our lives if we try to assess our significance in view of the big picture?

Yet, are we even justified to examine our activities and life on a much larger scale beyond our personal sphere? I believe the answer is both yes and no. No, if we strive for what Qohelet seeks. He drops hints of his ambition to be almost Godlike in seeking significance. He expresses disappointment in failing to make a major contribution to this world (Eccl 1:3–15) and in acknowledging human limitations (Eccl 3:9–14, 18–21; 8:16–17). In a way, we understand when we view him as perhaps one of the wisest men who ever lived (Eccl 1:16) and a king with virtually unlimited resources

---

20. Jesus concludes his statement about worry with these words (Matt 6:34): "So do not worry about tomorrow; for tomorrow will worry about itself. Each day has enough trouble of its own." At first glance, it may seem that Jesus confines the idea of carpe diem to one literal day where tomorrow denotes the very next day. That, I do not believe, is his intent. Rather, he exhorts his audience to focus on the concerns and challenges of the present, carpe diem. Earlier, he cautions not to worry about life in the broadest sense (Matt 6:25). Then he describes the grass as that "which is alive today and tomorrow is thrown into the furnace" in a figurative manner, not a literal twenty-four-hour period, connoting a short existence or a season (Matt 6:30b).

and opportunities (Eccl 1:12; 2:4–10). But he is still human and therefore bounded by his human nature.

The answer is affirmative to whether we ought to factor in the bigger picture if we submit to the frame narrator's admonition to fear God and to keep his commandments (Eccl 12:13b), mindful that he will hold us accountable for all that we do (Eccl 12:14). Distilling all his commandments into the two greatest—"You shall love the Lord your God with all your heart, and with all your soul, and with all your mind" and "You shall love your neighbor as yourself" (Matt 22:37–40)—we have a solid grasp of our stewardship to God. We fear or revere him through obedience. The larger picture would certainly encompass all our neighbors and it will also keep God and our accountability to him at center stage. When we experience carpe diem, we need to acknowledge God's grace in gifting us with satisfaction and enjoyment in the simple, ordinary things in life. This thankful attitude is not overt in Qohelet's writings. Even though we may not discern the connection between our lives and the big picture, we trust that God has integrated the two together. Qohelet himself acknowledges our human limitations about mysteries of the divine (Eccl 3:11). However, Qohelet does not completely disagree with the frame narrator when he writes, "remember your Creator" (Eccl 12:1a) especially in one's youth. But he does not specify what that remembrance entails.

Challenge of Carpe Diem in Old Age

The preceding discussion applies to much of our lives, especially when we pursue career and other things in life. But does our worldview change with the onset of old age, when we retire or when our growing awareness of the end becomes a constant companion?

Certainly, one thing we must bear in mind is Qohelet's admonition (Eccl 7:10) to avoid the question, "Why is it that the former days were better than these?" He advises that such a query does not align with wisdom. Wisdom does not dwell in the past and especially does not cling to the past in order to avoid dealing with the present. But what does "better" mean? Leaving the comparative unspecified invites the reader to make personal application. The characteristics of old age can make one recall with fondness and sadness the earlier years when we enjoyed the prime of health and vigor with the prospect of many years of adventure ahead of us.

Eighty-year-old Barzillai speaks for all us older folks when he refused David's invitation by declaring (2 Sam 19:35bcde), "Can I distinguish between good and bad? Or can your servant taste what I eat or what I drink? Or can I still hear the voice of men and women singing? Why then should your servant be an added burden to my lord the king?" We have lost the capacity of youth to engage fully in life with zest and to enjoy all the pleasures we hold precious. We fear being a burden to others, especially to those close to us.

The principle of carpe diem may seem beyond our grasp. What satisfaction and enjoyment can we experience hampered as we are by the undeniable symptoms of our declining years? Until the Lord calls us home, we must assume he has something in mind for each of us. We need to live in the present and maximize each day's potential. Other passages support this thought. "Teach us to number our days" (Ps 90:12a). The concept of "today" can bear this idea as well. After reading Isa 61:1–2a in the synagogue, Jesus proclaims, "Today this Scripture has been fulfilled in your hearing." (Luke 4:21b). He does not mean a literal twenty-four-hour period, but his physical presence signifies fulfillment of prophecy. In Heb 3:12–13, the writer exhorts: "Take care, brothers and sisters, that there will not be in any one of you an evil, unbelieving heart that falls away from the living God. But encourage one another every day, as long as it is still called 'today,' so that none of you will be hardened by the deceitfulness of sin." Here "today" connotes opportunity while it lasts, for however long, but will eventually cease. Thus, the present represents an opportunity to live out our lives as fully as we can on a day-to-day basis even if age restricts our options. This aligns with carpe diem. If God wills it, he gives us the gift of life, satisfaction, and even joy.

Of course, we will have to adjust what we regard as satisfaction and enjoyment. I used to run regularly covering several miles in a single stint and I frequented the local weight room. Now I walk and do body-weight exercises. My stamina and ability to recover from physical exertion have declined. I don't like it; but I have to accept my limitations.

The same principle applies to my ministry. I served as a full-time pastor and later as a full-time member of the faculty at a seminary. But now I have cut back to part-time teaching and feel some fatigue after each class. A pastor friend sharing my birth year told me a few years ago that his stamina had dramatically dwindled to the point where he had to step down. I still contribute meaningfully to prepare another generation of ministers, albeit in a reduced role. So long as I make the mental and psychological adjustment, I can still embrace carpe diem.

Looking Ahead to Our Future

Many in old age do not want to think about the future, rationalizing: "What future? What is there to look forward to?" Perhaps a sense of foreboding discourages them from doing so. But as Howard Hendricks, longtime professor, conference speaker, and author, said, "When your memories are more exciting than your dreams, you've begun to die." Dreams see the possibilities, look forward to the future with hope, activate the mind to conceive the next steps, and move the body to take action. Life is far from over; there are yet paths to trod. Dreams animate and excite.

An article recounts Hendricks's involvement with an 80-year-old desiring to learn Greek. The excerpt follows:

> He [Hendricks] beams when he tells the story of an 80-year-old who came to Dallas Theological Seminary wanting to learn Greek. "I said 'Are you sure?' He said, 'I am just fascinated by this stuff.'" After four years, the man was so accomplished in Greek that Hendricks hired him to teach freshmen. He became one of the seminary's most-loved professors until his retirement at the age of 93. It was this man's excitement, fascination and love of learning that got him studying the Bible in a new way.[21]

Imagine a man being excited, fascinated, and strongly motivated to learn a new language in his eighties who later teaches well into his nineties. Seminary studies demand physical stamina and mental acuity. Here is one older person undaunted by the challenges who directs his passion to aspire and to attain his lofty goal.

As an older person, to what do we aspire? Do we have clear goals and the drive to strive toward them? Whether we succeed or not is perhaps not as important as having a forward-looking orientation in life and the willingness to pursue our dreams. Life is worth living and we feel empowered. Then old age no longer drags us down although we may not have the energy and strength of a bygone era. So let us keep dreaming and plan accordingly. Let us take steps, however small or tentative. For once we stop dreaming,

---

21. Newcombs, "Howard Hendricks' 4 Bible Study Steps."

planning, and taking steps, we have chosen to pursue the one remaining option—we are waiting to die.

Wisdom: The End Better Than the Beginning

A very wise man, Qohelet, unequivocally declares: "A good name is better than good oil" (Eccl 7:1a), echoing Prov 22:1 ("A good name is to be more desired than great wealth; favor is better than silver and gold"), in order to explain why "the day of one's death is better than the day of one's birth" (Eccl 7:1b). Accrued after living a life that earns for the bearer a good reputation, a good name represents high social credit, especially in an honor-shame society. Usually that calls for exhibiting consistent character traits deemed admirable and accomplishments worthy of praise. The parallelism in Eccl 7:1 facilitates the analogy: as a good name is more precious than fine perfume, valuable in its own right, so death is more precious than birth. Birth offers potential of a life well-lived but it remains only a possibility until that life unfolds to confirm or not the promise. Death, however, marks the conclusion of a full and meaningful life. Of course, a person might dissipate innate abilities, favorable circumstances, and opportunities; but Qohelet does not consider this alternative. Thus, actualization is superior to potential.

"A house of mourning" (Eccl 7:2a) symbolizes the end of life. Mourning is the normal and expected emotion from loss and grief. The contrast with "a house of feasting" is clear enough but to prefer mourning over feasting may, at first glance, seem counterintuitive. But Eccl 7:4 provides the rationale: wisdom prefers mourning and foolishness prefers pleasure. In general, Qohelet views wisdom positively as a virtue in spite of its limitations; namely, it cannot prevent death (Eccl 2:13–16). The "house of feasting" seems to represent frivolous, shallow, and even hedonistic activity, something fools would not stop to think through but simple-mindedly engage in for the sake of gratification. Ecclesiastes 7:5–6 supports this idea. The expressions "song of fools" and "laughter of the fool" contrast with "rebuke of a wise person" and similar to the "crackling of thorn bushes under a pot," respectively, connoting something "meaningless" (Eccl 7:6). Here the term "meaningless/absurd" (*hebel*) appears to connote insubstantiality. Continuing, Qohelet reinforces the theme in Eccl 7:8 ("The end of a matter is better than its beginning; patience of spirit is better than arrogance of spirit"). Patience enables a person to see a matter to its logical conclusion even if it should be a protracted process. When the end arrives, the person's patience is confirmed and rewarded.

Expanding this basic idea of a long-term event nearing the end of its process to encompassing all of the journey of life, those of us in our twilight years should find strong affirmation that we can anticipate our end being better than our beginning. The best is yet to come. Rather than facing the anticlimax of our lives—tempting us to look backwards—we should view our final phase as the climax—something to look forward to. In the meantime, our focus should be cultivating a good name through our faithful service to the Lord and to others. We approach the finish line, maintaining our pace and not slacking. We want to finish well and hear our Lord's words of commendation.

A life well-lived offers its own reward and satisfaction. That seems like the ideal. But no one ever lived a perfect life devoid of mistakes and misfortune and, perhaps, a tinge of regret. However, Ecclesiastes is not written by a perfect person for readers who lead perfect lives. The prevailing worldview of this Wisdom book regards life as difficult, limiting, mysterious, and disappointing. Difficult because bad things happen to good people (Eccl 7:15); limiting because regardless of how wise and successful a person may be, they like the fool cannot prolong their lives (Eccl 2:14–16) and, in that sense, do not differ from beasts (Eccl 3:18–21); mysterious because no human can fully comprehend God and his ways (Eccl 3:11) nor can they meaningfully contribute to God's activities (Eccl 7:13) or discern the future (Eccl 7:14c); and disappointing because the wisest and most resource-rich person who ever lived still experiences keen disappointment and disillusionment when he surveys all that he has accomplished (Eccl 1:12—2:11). Sometimes life does not make much sense and logic does not always explain reality. Yet, we can still aspire to obtaining a good name.

A good name is our reward from the Lord as he confers his approval of our life and service. A good name also serves to encourage others who may be further back in their journey of life to remain faithful and true. Indeed, we and our twilight peers can mutually spur one another as we "see the day drawing near" (Heb 10:25d). What injects hope comes not from Qohelet but from the frame narrator, the second voice who, in forming a counter backdrop to the incessantly negative view on things in the majority of the book, offers a clear advocacy to one's whole duty in life—"fear God and keep his commandments, because this applies to every person" (Eccl 12:13b). Pursuing the two greatest commandments (Matt 22:37–40; Mark

12:29–31) would contribute to establishing a good name before the Lord, securing his approval.

In Filipino culture, an old person's birthday calls for, even demands, the proper celebratory activities, where relatives come, sometimes from overseas, to mark the significant milestone. One Filipina recalls her late grandmother's seventy-fifth, eightieth, and eighty-fifth birthdays, when the whole family gathered, some traveling from Canada, Dubai, and America to the Philippines. The grandmother was the star, all attention focused on her. Everyone, even non-family members, served her in whatever needs she had. The event seems more important than the birth of a child, doubtless a joyous occasion also. This reverence for the elderly serves as an analogy to Qohelet's view that the end is better than the beginning. Even though this grandmother led a challenging life raising ten children, in her later years she possessed enormous acquired honor.

Qohelet's Legacy

The recent passing of the actor Sean Connery spawns tributes from fellow actors and film producers and fans. As the original James Bond, Connery established a standard by which fans measure and compare all future actors playing the role.[22] Accolades recognize Connery's wit, sex appeal, and charisma. A number call him a legend.

In regard to one's legacy, a sociologist identifies important intangibles like values, beliefs, or attitudes that are passed down to a future generation and "is a summary of who we are and how we will be remembered should we die in this moment."[23] Some if not most of us think about our possible legacy, something about ourselves that lives on after our passing and that will impact others.

We find something that can represent Qohelet's legacy from the assessment by the frame narrator who shares (Eccl 12:9–10): "In addition to being wise, the Preacher also taught the people knowledge; and he pondered, searched out, and arranged many proverbs. The Preacher sought to find delightful words and to write words of truth correctly." It can be regarded

---

22. The first actor to play James Bond was Barry Nelson in a TV special broadcasted on CBS in 1954 as an episode of the *Climax! Mystery Theatre*.

23. Peticolas, a national speaker and expert on the topics of loss, emotional wounding, and unresolved grief, holds a PhD in sociology and has over twenty years' experience coaching people through major life challenges. See "What Is Your Legacy?"

as a eulogy given Qohelet's closing remarks about death (Eccl 12:5d–7) that may reflect his own impending situation and his evaluation of all his experimentation, accomplishments, and discoveries over a significant period of time (Eccl 2:1–11). If we assume that he reviews his observations, insights, and conclusions about life, humanity, and the human endeavor based, in large measure, on his own experiences, we can picture him toward the end of his life recording his thoughts, lessons, admonitions, and warnings in a carefully crafted treatise for the next generation. This particular observation about Qohelet comes from the frame narrator and not from him. Thus, we learn that Qohelet must have some regard for others and so makes the effort to benefit them.

Then Ecclesiastes sans the closing frame (Eccl 12:9–14) represents Qohelet's legacy, an intentional blessing to future generations who will experience what he has encountered but who will also be prepared to face the same challenges of transience, insubstantiality, and foulness. Life is not fair; plans may not pan out; frustration, disappointment, and enigma may arise. This is reality, sometimes raw and difficult. So do not be surprised. But along with the warning comes instruction, the imparting of wisdom—basically a "here's how to survive and to make the best of a tough situation." Qohelet offers two significant positive pointers: (1) a lofty view of God transcendent, inaccessible, and sovereign in authority, and (2) carpe diem as God's gift to humanity to enjoy.

To better appreciate Qohelet's worldview that impacts his legacy, we examine two aspects of his world and life. First, he contextualizes his life's work within the grand scheme of things (Eccl 1:3–11). He raises the question of significance: "What advantage does a person have in all his work which he does under the sun?" (Eccl 1:3) It is an existential question to which he fails to find a satisfactory answer. Essentially, he concludes—nothing: "All is futility!" (Eccl 1:2d). By futility, he means insubstantiality—what appears at first sight to be promising is, in reality, disappointing, lacking any substance or value. The secondary idea of transience is closely allied with a lack of value. Life is too short to make any significant contribution to the world. When he laments the passing of successive generations that leave the earth and its natural processes unaltered and perpetual (Eccl 1:4–10), we understand that he means humans can make no contribution that would change the world in any permanent fashion. Of course, we today might counter with examples of humanity's affecting the earth in irrevocable ways, for example, climate change due to pollution and the depletion of natural resources, as well as the extinction of various animal species due to human encroachment into natural habitats and over hunting. These forces are not operational in Qohelet's time. Nor are these modern changes positive or beneficial in contradiction to the good that Qohelet, I believe, has in mind. Then we might point to advances in technology and medicine that make life more comfortable and convenient and enable us to do things we cannot do before—the internet, for example, grants us unprecedented access to information and to one another anywhere in the world, and better medical care and effective treatment of diseases can lead to longer life spans. Of course, the downside of the internet is a too easy access to unwholesome websites and vulnerability to cyberattacks. Technological advances may be harnessed for the benefit of humanity or for perpetrating crime and conflict against one another (warfare has evolved with the use of ever-increasing sophistication of weaponry but the underlying reasons for armed conflict remain unchanged). It all depends on the intent and motivation of the user. As Scripture teaches, human nature harbors a propensity for evil and that has remained a fact of life regardless of the period in history.

The second aspect of Qohelet's world and life concerns his position and advantages. He is a king and teacher in some official capacity, endowed with superior wisdom compared to all previous rulers (Eccl 1:12–16). His potential to achieve noteworthy projects is enormous, and he can observe life, both his and that of others, and the world-at-large and draw meaningful insights. Hence, even if we struggle to accept his conclusion, that "all is futility," we cannot easily dismiss him. But we should query about the proper context in which to understand his thoughts and point of view. For that, we turn to the frame narrator.

He cautions readers to desist from trying to add to Qohelet's investigation and writings (Eccl 12:12) implying that nothing more can really be added and would, therefore, be wasted effort. Indeed, the frame narrator himself makes only a small but significant adjustment to the preceding writings in two short verses (Eccl 12:13–14). In admonishing readers to fear God and to keep his commandments, the frame narrator presents a compatible portrait of God with that of Qohelet's but with an important caveat—loving the Lord our God with our all implies a relationship, something Qohelet appears to lack. He fails to depict any prayer life. He offers no cries to God, no seeking the Lord. The closest he comes is in his admonition about entering the house of God (Eccl 5:1–7). Even then, however, he advises having a listening posture with at most few words spoken (Eccl 5:2c).

He discourages making vows but does not prohibit them, urging those who make vows to be sure to fulfill them (Eccl 5:4–6). Thus, prayer receives no emphasis.

Yet, Qohelet has gifted successive generations with considerable insights, admonitions, and warnings to prepare them to succeed in life, avoiding some pitfalls, navigating through challenges, finding blessings where possible, and expecting difficulties, incongruities, and enigmas so that they will not be overly shocked or overwhelmed.

The old people of Malaysia, the Kachin tribe of Myanmar, and the Philippines represent a modern parallel to Qohelet in having the privilege to teach the younger generation. They pass on cultural values and insights and religious practices. Reaching old age is an acquired honor that demands respect and a listening ear. And the honorable thing to do is to take the role of teacher, guide, advisor, and role model seriously.

Our Legacy

Combining the collective wisdom of Qohelet and the frame narrator, we can develop and implement our own legacy. Our significance comes through impacting the lives of others both in the present and in the future. Our core values, convictions, and practices get transferred to them and so, in a sense, we live on through their lives.

If we take a page literally from Qohelet's approach as the frame narrator has summarized (Eccl 12:9–10), we note a few things to bear in mind as we strive to bless others. First, we ask ourselves, "Have I gained wisdom and knowledge from my life experiences that are worth passing on to others?" We ought to offer something substantial and beneficial. Perhaps we suffered a mishap, a tragedy, or a failure. What lessons we gain from those difficult events might be crafted as a warning of things to avoid or to keep in mind should someone else face similar difficulties. What insights we accrue from the challenges and difficulties may prove instructive. Guidance and teachings from others—our mentors, teachers, or parents—that we confirm to be valid or have benefited from can likewise be passed on to the next generation. Second, Qohelet researches and then composes many proverbs, pithy and memorable snippets of universal truths, that he gives to his readers. He demonstrates intentionality, forethought, and careful composition of his counsel and advice. Then he finds an avenue through which to communicate. As a monarch, he enjoys a ready platform and receptive audience. On our part, we survey our potential platform and potential audience and, before that important step, we should evaluate our credibility. Would people respect us enough to give us a hearing? We also ask, Who may benefit, and do we have a viable relationship with them? Third, Qohelet's counsel is characterized as "words of truth." There is both a moral and informational component to his teaching. Known as "Teacher/Preacher," he enjoys great public esteem and respect. More than simply guiding our mentees to lead productive lives, we want to influence them morally. Such an objective, of course, demands that we ourselves model what we want them to become. With the added admonition from the frame narrator to fulfill our responsibilities to God (Eccl 12:13), knowing of our accountability to him (Eccl 12:14), we exhort our charges to nurture their relationship with their Lord. We influence them by our personal example and by our instruction and counsel.

One more observation about Qohelet concerns his careful selection of just the right words to couch his advice, teaching, exhortation, and warning. This ancient practice is as pertinent today as it was in his day. An article entitled, "Finding the Right Words in a Crisis," originally addressed to business leaders, applies equally well to us ordinary citizens.[24] Word choice is absolutely critical not only in crisis situations—the operating premise of the article—but also in other circumstances where important information must be conveyed persuasively. The writer makes a noteworthy observation: "Many economists and CEOs today swear that words are the most important tool in a world where 'command and control' leadership has given way to power by persuasion."[25] He presents four fundamental principles to guide us in crafting our message: (1) replace long words with short ones, (2) find analogies, (3) personalize the crisis, and (4) observe the rule of three. Since the first principle is self-explanatory, I will offer a summary of the other three. Finding analogies is the practice of relating what may be new or unfamiliar with what is familiar to our audience for ready comprehension. Jesus employs analogy through parables using familiar, commonplace circumstances to teach. Adapting the principle of personalizing the crisis to non-crisis situations, we share our personal stories and experiences in order to illustrate and also to move our listener. People relate to stories, especially those that are our stories. We gain not only their attention but also their empathy. As a result, they would be more open to our ideas and

---

24. Gallo, "Finding the Right Words."
25. Gallo, "Finding the Right Words," §3.

more willing to adopt our suggestions. Finally, the rule of three pertains to making no more than three points for better memory retention. I conclude this discussion on word choice with the article's final thought: "Like a virus, words are infectious. They can instill fear and panic or facilitate understanding and calm. Above all, they can spark action. So choose them carefully."[26] Words are powerful either for good or evil. A modern example of how words can sway a nation to evil is Adolf Hitler.[27] A counter example of using words for good is Hitler's contemporary, Winston Churchill.[28] To ensure that our words have the proper effect, we use the frame narrator's admonition of fearing God and keeping his commandments (Eccl 12:13) to guide us. Our objective is to pass on to others that admonition in hopes that they too will embrace it as we have.

Thus, like Qohelet let us find "words of truth" (Eccl 12:10). This strategy calls for careful planning and review. Reflecting back on our lives, we strive to identify key thoughts, insights, and lessons learned that may be potentially beneficial to others. We may elect to make notes or to journal in order to sort out our thoughts and to organize them in some coherent manner. Indeed, we can take a page from Qohelet's writings. His reflections reveal various modes of expression—general observations (Eccl 5:13—6:2), narrative of his own experiences along with the attendant conclusion (Eccl 2:1–11), admonition (Eccl 5:1–4), advice (Eccl 7:21–22), warning (Eccl 5:5–6), brief stories of specific but anonymous individuals that illustrate a point (Eccl 4:13–16; 9:13–18), promise (Eccl 2:26ab), and proverb (Eccl 10:8–20). We may not be as articulate and literary as Qohelet nor as broad and varied in our experiences; but we have something of value to pass on.

Most importantly, we should emulate Qohelet's transparency. He is completely open, honest, hiding nothing, not even the negative aspects of his life. He struggles with *hebel*, his term for insubstantiality, transience, and foulness. His personal resources, position, and wisdom motivate him to aspire to great achievements, which he attains (Eccl 2:4–10), but those only deepen his disappointment and frustration leaving him empty, feeling like a complete failure (Eccl 2:11). Then the profound awareness of his mortality sensitizes him to his helplessness to change his fate (Eccl 2:14b–23). He can only conclude (Eccl 5:15): "As he came naked from his mother's womb, so he will return as he came. He will take nothing from the fruit

---

26. Gallo, "Finding the Right Words," §27.
27. See, for example, Kanfer, "Architect of Evil," 48–50.
28. Gilbert, *Churchill, the Power of Words*.

of his labor that he can carry in his hand." He likens a person's activities as laboring for the wind (5:16) and depicts people's lives as "darkness with great irritation, sickness, and anger" (Eccl 5:17b). Qohelet sounds overly harsh and raw, threatening to drag his readers down to despondency, disillusionment, and cynicism. Why bother trying to do anything if it only leads to frustration and disappointment?

But in spite of his bleak outlook, he never gives up nor does he counsel his readers to quit. The critical factor that safeguards his sanity and permits him to continue his labor, as I see it, is his high regard for God. He acknowledges God's sovereign authority in personal affairs and favor to those who please him (Eccl 2:24–26; 3:12–13; 5:18–20; 6:2; 7:13–14), that everyone will give an account to him (Eccl 3:15, 17; 11:9d), that proper decorum must be observed in his presence (Eccl 5:1–7), and that he and his activities transcend human comprehension and interference (Eccl 1:15; 3:11c, 14; 7:13–14; 8:17; 11:5). Qohelet also contrasts God's eternal works (Eccl 3:14) with human finiteness in terms of their labor and potential profit (Eccl 2:14b–23).

Like Qohelet we may not always understand God's mysterious ways and may experience disappointment or even despondency, but do we maintain a high view of God? Do we acknowledge his sovereign authority and submit to his plans for us when he does not appear to meet our requests and hopes? Will we influence our younger contemporaries to harbor deep reverence for the Lord? Only if we ourselves do and model it.

Then Qohelet calls on the youth to remember their Creator (Eccl 12:1a) before the onset of old age followed by death (Eccl 12:1b–7). We wonder why the tone of this admonition sounds like a warning. A ticking biological clock imposes a sense of urgency—better remember your Creator while you still can. That seems to imply that it would be easier to do so in one's youth. The ravages of old age may make one forget or even resent God. But the lifelong habit of revering the Lord, as Qohelet demonstrates, may continue into the final stage of life when it is more challenging. This attitude may be our most powerful gift to others—when all discernable outward signs do not confirm the Lord's goodness in our lives due to struggles in the late stages of our lives and we still hold onto our integrity and praise him. We may encourage them to cling to God in their times of trouble and to continue doing so when they enter old age.

The frame narrator adds the crucial admonition to complement Qohelet and even to enhance the Teacher's contribution. Although his comments are brief, his words provide the much-needed balance and finishing touches to the book overall. His key thought concerns our relationship with God through fearing him and obeying him (Eccl 12:13). The relational dimension emerges forcefully when we summarize God's commandments through the two greatest (Matt 22:36–40)—we love the Lord our God with our entire being and love our neighbor as ourselves. A careful reading of Qohelet's writings yields no similar affirmation. Instead, we find his references to fearing God (Eccl 3:14; 5:7; 7:18; 8:12–13). But even though both writers use the same term for fear,[29] the curious impression is that their use differs. Qohelet does not seem to have a personal, intimate relationship with God; there is a sense of reverential distance, even dread at the possibility of incurring God's anger (Eccl 5:6–7). To be fair, however, the frame narrator does not explicitly mention a relationship; it is only inferred from his admonition to keep the commandments. But it must be that relationship with the Lord and the intentional connection with others that will sustain us in our final years, where we view our lives as significant and potentially impactful. Our later years need not whimper away in resignation because of the lessening of our strength, stamina, and faculties. God continues to value us as do those whom we have affected in some beneficial manner.

These relationships, then, constitute to a large extent our legacy. What will people remember about us? Will they be inspired by our love for the Lord by modeling an intimate relationship with him? Will our prayer life and devotions showcase that vertical dynamic? A story from Africa illustrates this point. A group of devout villagers regularly go out into the thicket for prayer, each person claiming a chosen spot. In due time, the path leading to the particular spot becomes worn with the constant treading on the grass, serving as a visible confirmation that the person has maintained the habit of prayer. But the one who slacks off from this spiritual discipline eventually has an accuser of their delinquency—the grass growing back and covering their trail. Then fellow believers gently remind the slacker: "Brother, the grass grows on your path." Our spiritual practices become evident to others, encouraging or discouraging them to follow suit. Nurtured by these habits, our relationship with the Lord will be evident. Should they be lifelong, our consistency serves to inspire others to remain faithful to the Lord. This, then, represents a significant aspect of our legacy. In some ways,

---

29. Both the verb form (Eccl 3:14; 5:7; 8:12 [second incidence]; 12:13) and the adjectival form (Eccl 7:18; 8:12 [first incidence]; 8:13) appear.

being an older disciple, especially a lifelong one, carries more weight as a testament to faithfulness, both the Lord's and ours.

Chapter 6

Concluding Thoughts

As researchers and people around the globe recognize, the world's population is aging, where the percentage of the demographic passing the somewhat arbitrary threshold of 65 years of age is increasing. In some countries, particularly in Asia, the aging rate is higher than for other regions. According to some projections, the total number of old people will double by 2050. With the decrease in birth rates and the increase of life expectancy, at least in developed countries due to advances in medical care and technology, aging occupies the attention and concern of governments, the tech industry, and society in general. Achieving longer life moves somewhat to the margins to give higher priority to quality of life throughout people's life span, maintaining good health and functionality and providing elderly care. Correspondingly, the level of interest among average citizens has also jumped as they themselves, a family member, or a close acquaintance (friend or neighbor) enter this category. The impact is direct or, at the very least, indirect.

Focusing our attention on Asia, we note, for example, that according to the World Bank, China's aging population passed the 13 percent mark a couple of years ago, although the nation trails Japan and some other countries in that regard.[1] Another study, however, places the percentage at nearly 19 percent.[2] By comparison, the comparable percentages are 30 percent in Japan, 14 percent in Singapore, 15 percent in Thailand, 20 percent in Hong

---

1. World Bank, "Population Ages 65."
2. Liu, "China's 'Silver' Economy Grows."

Kong SAR, and 17 percent in the US.[3] In exploring ways to address quality of life for the elderly, China promotes tourism for retirees who now have plenty of leisure time.[4] Although this strategy features an economic aspect, the primary focus centers on the physical and mental health of seniors through travel and entertainment. The specifics are not the main concern here but the fact the government makes the effort to improve quality of life for the elderly proves significant. Only when the population ages noticeably would society respond.

BIBLICAL HERMENEUTICS OF AGEISM

Of the set of biblical hermeneutical principles that emerges from a survey of Scripture in chapter 2, let me highlight a few that especially speaks to us older readers powerfully.

Principle 1

If the believing community regards a member as older, that member should read and interpret Scripture to see how they may fulfill their role as a "father" or "mother," thereby leaving a legacy. The kind of wisdom (inferred from reading Job) that older folks should have and display is theological and spiritual; and we must pass that wisdom on to the next generation so that they too revere the Lord.

This principle comes from 1 Tim 5:1–2. Paul distinguishes the older from the younger members of the believing community. Even though he does not specify a particular age other than what he states in 1 Tim 5:9 for widows qualified for support at 60 and above, the ambiguity invites us to interpret and make our own application. In fact, each community decides for itself who is treated as the older generation and who are younger. In Asian cultures, often society addresses the older folks as "uncle" or "auntie," comparable to Paul's admonition. How do people discern to what category a person belongs? Primarily the appearance—white hair, wrinkles, a weather-beaten face, slow gait especially when aided by a cane, stooped posture. How one spends the day can prove quite revealing. In my neighborhood, the elderly sit at tables in a hawker center, something unique to Singapore,

3. World Bank, "Population Ages 65."
4. Tuo et al., "Cultural Factors and Senior Tourism," 1–9.

and spend nearly the entire day eating, drinking, and chatting with their peers. This is their daily routine including weekends.

This principle of differentiating the generations within the community nurtures a collectivist mindset and dynamic. Believers constitute a family with God as Father. We share common beliefs and practices. We fulfill the divine mandate to love one another. A sampling shows how frequent the command appears in the NT (John 13:34–35; 15:12, 17; Rom 12:10; 13:8; 1 Thess 3:12; 4:9; 1 Pet 4:8; 1 John 3:11, 23; 2 John 5). Viewing the elderly as fathers and mothers implies regarding them as the source of wisdom, a ready resource for consultation and advice, respecting them as the way to show them love. They in turn have the responsibility of teaching, guiding, encouraging, and admonishing, as their way of showing the younger people love. Loving relationships are mutual but how they love one another depends in large measure on which generation they belong to and what they can offer to others. Everyone participates; no expectation on anyone exceeds their capacity.

Utilizing Paul's teaching about Christ's body, we note some truths (1 Cor 12:4–7): "Now there are varieties of gifts, but the same Spirit. And there are varieties of ministries, and the same Lord. There are varieties of effects, but the same God who works all things in all persons. But to each one is given the manifestation of the Spirit for the common good." The empowering Holy Spirit resides in us all, old and young. He manifests himself through each one of us for the common good. The Spirit does not discriminate; all members serve the Lord through the gifts bestowed by the Spirit and ministries directed by the same God. The elderly are never too old to take an active role in the body. In the rest of the chapter, Paul argues that every part has an essential role and is very much needed by all the others. The old need other old members and the young members; the young need other young members as well as the old members. Let me cite Paul (1 Cor 12:13): "For by one Spirit we were all baptized into one body, whether Jews or Greeks, whether slaves or free, and we were all made to drink of one Spirit." Giftings, ministries, and roles differ, but everyone is equally part of the body; age does not lessen someone's importance.

However, an age-related question arises: does our role change within the body as we get older, especially when our energy level decreases, our physical stamina lessens, and perhaps even our mental acuity loses some sharpness? Paul offers no indication that the Spirit's gifting and working within us depend on age. The volume of ministry may lessen with reduced capacity; but the kind of ministry remains, for the Spirit works within us. We depend on him and not solely on ourselves. Yet, Paul indicates a potential change in inter-member relationships in the Timothy passage. As we enter old age, people's perception of us changes, regarding us as a "father" or "mother" (the Asian equivalent of uncle and aunt). Thus, we gain ascribed honor with age. However, acquired honor comes only if we fulfill our roles well.[5] Unlike the principles of ancient society where honor is heavily gender-dependent with the male gaining honor by some virtuous achievement outside the home and the female avoiding shame through some compromising association or activity and staying at home,[6] the honorable member of Christ's body, whether male or female, aspires to the same honor by respecting one another in loving relationships. As an older member, we gain added honor provided, of course, we fulfill our stewardship within the community. The added honor appears to imply assuming a more caring role as a nursing mother and exhorting, encouraging, and imploring as a father to his children to live in a manner worthy of God (1 Thess 2:7, 11–12a).

Principle 2

Interpret the biblical characters' explicitly mentioned progression in age as a theological benchmark. The characters' ages and progressive aging serve as a narrative time marker to give readers the sense of God's faithfulness to his promises and of the gradual unfolding of his plans over the years.

The realization that the advancing or advanced ages of the biblical characters function as a theological and narrative time marker in order to give a panoramic sweep of God's movement in and through their lives, often inclusive of the broader involvement in their people's or nation's history, contributes to interpreting the larger picture of God's purpose and intervention in human affairs. Portrayed as the Lord of history and people groups, God exercises sovereign authority as he fulfills his word, often in

---

5. Studying honor and shame in the ancient Mediterranean world, Malina views the woman's honor under the protection and control of her husband and by staying within boundaries of acceptable behavior (*New Testament World*, 47–48). According to Malina, widows regain lost honor through remarriage in order to be under a man. In God's family, however, God himself is the head and Paul encourages remarriage only if the young widow stands in danger of violating their allegiance to Christ and getting into mischief (1 Tim 5:11–14).

6. Malina, *New Testament World*, 49–50.

the context of covenant promises. Many of these characters have a prophetic or some other strategic role that impacts many others. That explains why their stories form part of the biblical narrative. Concurrently, their stories show how the events also affect them personally.

Reading that a character's age makes significant theological statements prompts us to reflect in an analogous fashion on the possible theological message our advanced age makes to our contemporaries and time. Although we do not have the particular roles these men and women have—prophet, ruler, administrator, or some other public office—their personal traits and, to some degree, their particular challenge may resonate with us. We share the same God and similar human strengths and frailties. What is God declaring through our long lives? What significant theological truths emerge through our testimony? Do his faithfulness and constancy shine through? Can we confirm his abiding presence as Immanuel? Do our stories reveal the victories and failures we have experienced, providing valuable lessons as the Lord continually teaches and molds us progressively more into the image of his Son?

What we must understand and utilize is that our old age is an advantage serving as a platform to proclaim a theological truth because of our stage in life. Long life is a gift from above. Because God never makes mistakes and acts according to his plans and purpose, leaving nothing to random chance, we view this latter portion of life as a golden opportunity to serve and honor our Lord. At the very least, we find ourselves in a similar vantage point as Joseph, who surveys all the intervening years from youth sold by his brothers into slavery up to and including the time he as Egypt's prime minister saves his extended family from a global famine and then announces to his brothers (Gen 50:20–21ab): "As for you, you meant evil against me, but God meant it for good in order to bring about this present result, to keep many people alive. So therefore, do not be afraid; I will provide for you and your little ones." Do we discern patterns and imprints of God's presence and intervention over the course of our long lives as Joseph does? Are we able to explain the significance of those patterns to others?

At our present juncture, we can survey all the years leading up to the present and gain perspective and insight into the significance of the various events and people that we encounter. We may identify interwoven threads, the interconnections between experiences that, at the time, do not appear related to other experiences. These threads give strong testimony to God's activity and the unfolding of his will and intervention, demonstrating his wisdom and love. Thus, reminiscing and reflecting represent an important spiritual discipline for the elderly. If we have journaled through the years, our recorded musings serve as an effective memory aid and rereading our writings triggers mental images and past emotions whereby we essentially relive our past. We recall past disappointments and celebrations, sadness and joy, fears and eager anticipations. We connect the dots and confirm God's guidance and sovereign intervention.

I recall the invitation the board of elders extended to me to join the pastoral team. I was totally surprised, not expecting the offered opportunity. At the time, I was engaged in advanced studies preparing for a career in theological education. I envisioned myself as a professor. I did not see myself as a pastor, harboring a preconceived notion of what such a person looked and acted like. I thought the pastorate would lead me away from my clear objective, a detour that would prevent me from fulfilling my dream. But after much prayer and discussion with various people including my family, I sensed God's directive to shepherd his flock. Hence, I pastored the congregation for a number of years. But upon completing my studies, I initiated the search for a teaching post. Only after I taught for a little while did I realize the necessity of having pastoral experience. Most of my students are preparing for the pastorate. What credibility would I have before them if I never served as a pastor? None. A purely academic background falls well short of being a fruitful teacher who can share with his students the tough lessons learned through the triumphs and failures of the ministry. Looking back, I now see clearly God's wisdom in preparing me each step of the way. I lack the necessary wisdom and insight in order to make informed decisions on my own that facilitate movement forward. Thankfully, I submitted to the Lord and, even though not fully appreciating it at the time, I gained the experience that built up my credibility. Reflection deepens insight. The elderly have this vantage point that younger people do not have.

Principle 3

The narrative and its emphasis are the determinative factors for discerning whether a character's recorded age plays an important role in the story or not. Even if a character's age does not play an important role in the narrative, it may still offer valuable insights into a person's character trait (for example, faithfulness over the years) so long as the reader does not subvert the narrative's major points in such character studies.

This principle seeks to avoid blatant moralizing of the text which disregards the context and the major thrust of the passage. Scripture portrays God as the main actor even if the narrative does not explicitly mention his involvement.[7] Reading the biblical text should lead to a deeper understanding of God, his character, purpose, activities, and interaction with people. Conviction to regard him as our Lord worthy of worship arises. The opportunity to know the Lord intimately prompts us to nurture a relationship with him.

Scripture is a theological document. The biblical narrative puts the spotlight on God. All other aspects of the narrative, including the human characters, support God as the main actor. The primary objective of the reader is to learn more about God, how he accomplishes his purpose, and the nature of his interaction with human characters. Even though God is eternal and can accomplish any task spontaneously, when he enters into the narrative, he inserts himself into the time frame of the world without disrupting the flow of time.[8] He maps his plans and the accomplishment of his purpose into the unfolding of history and the timeline of people. The inclusion of any human character, people or nation, and event contributes to the divine portrait being drawn. The reader strives to discern the significance of each element in relation to God. The narrator may state a character's age and length of life or something about their traits. Even if the stated fact catches the reader's attention, they need to subsume that element under the major thrust of the narrative by asking why the narrator mentions it and how it contributes to crafting the main point. Given the intentionality of the narrator where anything included or omitted reflects his streamlined approach (extraneous material could make it difficult to identify the main point), if a character's age or length of life appears in the text, we may assume the mentioned fact serves an important narrative

---

7. As scholars and commentators observe, the book of Esther omits any explicit mention of God or his name. Huey, for example, explains the omission as the product of God's hiddenness in judgment against the exiled Jews for their wayward behavior whereby he withdrew and remained silent ("Esther," 4:793). Proposing a much more imaginative solution to explain the absence of God's name, Gordis posits that Esther represents a unique genre—a Jewish writer masquerading as a gentile scribe of the Persian court composed a chronicle, that is, Esther ("Religion, Wisdom and History," 375–78). The writer's objective is to present a supposedly neutral account in order to promote the festival of Purim, the one feast not mentioned in the Torah.

8. The exception occurs when Joshua fights against the Amorite coalition at Gibeon. In response to Joshua's request, God stops the movements of the sun and moon for about a day to permit the complete slaughter of the enemy (Josh 10:12–14).

Concluding Thoughts

purpose. We ask how age or length of life relates to God's program. Does it affect the relationship between God and the character? If so, how so?

In asking such questions, we maintain the spotlight on the passage's main point and on God. We are not ignoring the details of the narrative; we discern their proper place and role in the narrative, assuming they make meaningful contributions to the storytelling. If, however, a particular detail strikes us forcefully, we ask why it resonates with us. Does it speak to our particular situation? If we affirm that, we can explore the ramifications with a view to the bigger picture and not ignore the overall movement of the narrative. Will we find parallels between the situation back then to our present circumstances? What do we learn about God and his movement through human affairs from studying the human character? Do our findings suggest something similar or analogous to God's involvement in our own lives?

Joseph's progressive aging, for example, punctuates his story and serves as a detail we older readers readily notice. The years between his initial enslavement and his interpretation of Pharaoh's dreams must have been very frustrating, anxious, and seemingly hopeless. Those of us who experienced years of frustration, a sense of life quickly slipping by without much meaning, and all the while aging, can more readily empathize with Joseph than a younger reader. We are more sensitive in our reading, wondering like Joseph may have whether we wasted our lives from missed opportunities or not getting the right breaks (Joseph could have been released from prison sooner if the chief cupbearer remembered, Gen 40:23). But because the narrative does not recount events in real time, Joseph's story moves rather quickly, too quickly for some readers to see things from Joseph's perspective. It is similar to thirty-minute TV shows that cover a few days or more with the problem faced by the characters solved before the half-hour mark.

From the perspective of the story overall, however, we see that those seemingly lost years align with God's purpose and timing to save his people from the famine and to keep his covenant promise to Jacob by placing Joseph in Egypt ahead of time. But why does God permit the betrayal by the brothers and the years of enslavement and imprisonment? Why could he not have Joseph go to Egypt as a free man, sparing him the hardship? The narrative does not explain. We might conjecture that the hardship toughened Joseph for his future role. But the narrative informs us that at no time does God ever abandon Joseph. In fact, the divine favor on him is evident to Potiphar (Gen 39:2–6) and the jailer (Gen 39:20–23), prompting both men to entrust Joseph with major responsibilities. He carries out his charges effectively, demonstrating his abilities and substantiating his trustworthiness. These qualities will serve him well when pharaoh appoints him the prime minister. We surmise that those years are not wasted but serve to prepare Joseph for significant leadership. Of course, he does not appreciate that until much later when he reviews the intervening years (Gen 50:20).

We older readers stand at a similar juncture as Joseph to review our lives and draw some conclusions. Can we discern God's intervention and timing in our lives? Do we understand that his program takes years to unfold, perhaps the entirety of our lives? Any resentment or bitterness Joseph may have harbored dissipates. In our old age can we make peace with others as Joseph does with his brothers? Joseph's story is really God's story as he superintends over the fate of his covenant people and using Egypt, a world power, to accomplish his purpose.

Principle 4

As stated previously, *the principle of suspicion that characterizes feminist and ecological readings of Scripture does not apply to our investigation of the biblical hermeneutics of ageism. The major argument for excluding this principle is that a survey of the spiritual and moral requirements of God's people throughout Bible history in both testaments yields no discernable differentiation between the older and younger members of the covenant community.* God holds equally accountable old and young. He does not consider the elderly's declining vigor, health, mental faculties, or other aspects of their late stage in life. Using a colloquialism, God does not cut old people any slack. They must maintain spiritual and moral excellence throughout all of life. Hence, any reading of Scripture's demands on God's people apply equally to all.

Reviewing the Ten Commandments,[9] the only commandment that may not apply to the elderly is the fifth ("Honor your father and your mother, so that your days may be prolonged on the land which the Lord your God gives you," Exod 20:12). Likely, the parents of the elderly have died and the elderly have already lived a long life.[10] However, we can still

---

9. Longman explains how we moderns should understand and submit to the Ten Commandments (*Making Sense of the Old Testament*, 111–23).

10. The generations preceding Abraham lived protracted lives compared to later generations. Haran, Abraham's brother, predeceased his father (Gen 11:27–28). Conceivably some children died before their parents. But the Ten Commandments only enter into

Concluding Thoughts

honor the memories of our deceased parents. For example, my mother was a cultured lady, refined and gentle. She never raised her voice and raised her son to be a gentleman. Out of love and respect for her, I still try to live up to her expectations and standards, many years after her passing.

Now the Fourth Commandment about keeping the Sabbath holy by ceasing all the normal labor of the other six days may or may not be relevant for the elderly who no longer engage in the work of their younger days. However, the intent of this commandment requires even the elderly to observe the Sabbath acceptably. It represents a time of remembrance and dedication to the Lord.

Thus, the Ten Commandments, summarizing the moral law, applies to old and young, not only in Israel's time but also in ours today. God holds us all accountable for observing all the commandments, the moral law.

Principle 5

Read and interpret Scripture to resist the Adversary in spiritual warfare giving particular attention to the vulnerabilities inherent with old age.

A number of my older colleagues, some retired but still active, suffer with various ailments, physical, mental, emotional, or some combination. They struggle to fulfill their ministry responsibilities. One has trouble thinking clearly because of COVID, making it difficult to prepare for his sermons, and another's vertigo cast doubt on his availability to attend meetings. Neither individual nor their coworkers explicitly suspect attacks from the enemy. But spiritual warfare represents a constant threat, particularly for the Lord's servants in strategic roles. I suffered depression a few years ago when I stepped down from my full-time teaching ministry. I felt like the passenger at the station who just missed the departing train when the following semester began. Everyone else, it seemed, was eagerly anticipating the new term. I wondered about my future and about my identity, so closely did I associate my work with my sense of worth. The Adversary can easily weaponize my uncertainties and emotions against me and paralyze my usefulness. I could have easily resented God or questioned his love for me.

As an older person, I am vulnerable. Three factors, however, provide a defense against spiritual attacks. One, my wife remains my most important

---

Jewish history in Moses's day when life spans have dropped significantly to 70 years or 80 in exceptional cases (Ps 90:10, with the associated title "a prayer of Moses the man of God"), long after Abraham.

ally and companion. She accurately diagnosed my previous condition and guided me out of my despondency. Two, I continue to read Scripture, realizing it harbors no age-based bias. From it I find assurance of God's continued love and faithfulness and also of his expectations of me unabated. I am still his servant even if my responsibilities change or diminish. So I must discern what those are and fulfill them. And three, my missions organization has no retirement policy; I can serve with them for as long as I desire or am able to. The organization represents a support network of like-minded people intent on the common goal of global missions.

In spiritual warfare, Jesus himself depends heavily on Scripture to resist the fiery darts of the Tempter, repeatedly citing, "it is written" (Matt 4:1–10; Luke 4:1–12; for the third temptation, Luke portrays Jesus responding, "It has been stated"). As his disciples, we follow his example. The Adversary may taunt us: "You are too old to obey or to serve the Lord." "You are useless, why bother honoring the Lord any longer?" "You are retired from your corporate career; you are also retired from your ministry at church; God cannot use you anymore." "Why don't you ask God for a young, vigorous body and sharp mind to better serve him?" "How can God possibly love you if he doesn't heal you of your age-related ailments?"

Can we rally ourselves into framing a viable defense? Do we cite Scripture, citing both the commands we must obey (for example, Eph 4:26–27) and the promises we must claim (for example, Jas 4:7)? Do we pray for strength to resist, confident in Jesus as our intervening High Priest (Heb 2:17–18; 4:14–16; 10:19–23)? In his time of testing in Gethsemane, Jesus fervently prays and urges his disciples to pray so they do not succumb to temptation (Matt 26:36–45; Mark 14:32–41; Luke 22:39–46). Furthermore, Scripture admonishes us to participate in a believing community for mutual encouragement (Heb 10:24–25) and to put on the armor of God in standing firm against the Adversary's schemes (Eph 6:10–17). Everyone, regardless of age, struggles with personal vulnerabilities that the Tempter can exploit. This divinely provided defense serves the old and the young; all must use it in order to secure the victory.

ECCLESIASTES

Reading this book requires caution. Qohelet's obsession with death dominants his thoughts making it somewhat dangerous for the reader, especially if they are impressionable. Of course, some of the elderly may be similarly obsessed. But uncertainty surrounds Qohelet's age, although his reflections about his past projects and achievements suggest a later stage in life. There is no explicit statement of age. His angst about death stems from a philosophical point of view rather than from personally struggling with the ravages of the last stage of life. He laments his human limitations—despite being wise he faces death just like the fool and wild beasts, so has no advantage over them, and he must leave the fruit of his labor to someone else after his passing. He observes the contrast between the enduring work of God and human finiteness.

We notice no effort by Qohelet to remedy his situation and point of view, seemingly resigned, grudgingly accepting the raw reality of life. He does not pray to God for comfort or for intervention to change his life. And he does not discuss his concerns with others, probably thinking that, since he is wiser than any of his contemporaries, it would be futile. We readers, especially the elderly, can easily share in his gloomy perspective and feel helpless, even hopeless, to change anything about our fate. Death is inevitable and for some of us it may be imminent.

Although Qohelet holds a lofty view of God, he reveals no evidence of a relationship with the Lord. Apparently, he does not pray. However, he advises anyone entering the house of God to go with a listening posture and limiting one's speech (Eccl 5:1–3). What may explain his not seeking God is his two-tier cosmology—all his experiences, observations, and insights emerge from his interaction with all that is "under the sun," a prominent motif. What lies above where God resides and operates remains a mystery. Qohelet views God as remote although he controls everything on earth. His admonition to fear God (Eccl 3:14; 5:7; 7:18) might be rendered as dread in the context of judgment. But in other passages he mentions fear in the sense of reverence (Eccl 8:12–13), the same thought expressed by the frame narrator (Eccl 12:13).

Whereas Qohelet's two-tier cosmology conforms to that of the rest of Scripture, yet we read David's prayers, especially the laments, and realize that he believes that God cares and responds to his servant's pleas for deliverance. The contrast in attitude and conduct between the two men is striking. Fear and desperation mark David's life and, no doubt, grief about his son Absalom. Yet, David experiences joy and celebration when he brings the ark of the covenant to Jerusalem and whenever he goes to the tabernacle. He never loses hope nor does he ever give up on God as Qohelet seems to have done. How do we explain the difference between the two?

Both live within the same period of redemptive history, that is, before the first Advent, Pentecost, and the completion of the NT that identifies Jesus Christ as the one meditator between God and humans.

Instead of following Qohelet's example, we should follow David's. Encouraged by the knowledge that we have a meditator with the Father, we pray when facing various life challenges, even that of old age. We need not resign ourselves to our fate. As Immanuel, God's abiding presence means that we are not alone.

Yet, when we read (Heb 4:14–16):

> Therefore, since we have a great high priest who has passed through the heavens, Jesus the Son of God, let's hold firmly to our confession. For we do not have a high priest who cannot sympathize with our weaknesses, but One who has been tempted in all things just as we are, yet without sin. Therefore let's approach the throne of grace with confidence, so that we may receive mercy and find grace for help at the time of our need.

We may respond, "Yes, but." Jesus dies young. He never experiences old age even by the standards of his time. So how can he possibly empathize with our struggles with old age? However, where we can find common ground is his anticipation of his impending death on the cross and the elderly seeing their approaching end. Although his death has redemptive implications and he willingly dies, he can look beyond death to his resurrection. Does the farsightedness that sees past death that characterizes Jesus also describe us? If so, then the gloom and bitterness associated with death lessen in our end stage. Faith sees beyond death to life in the presence of the Lord forever.

Qohelet complains about the necessity of passing on the fruits of his labor to someone else after his death. He prefers to enjoy it himself longterm but death interrupts. Does that thinking appear selfish? What about passing an inheritance to the children? Two thoughts come to mind in response to the question: one, Qohelet does not indicate that he has ever had children, and two, he compares favorably with the wealthy of today who refuse to give their children a sizable inheritance for fear of spoiling them.[11] In an interview, Bill Gates states: "It's not a favor to kids to have them have huge sums of wealth. It distorts anything they might do, creating their own

---

11. A current trend among a number of the wealthy or celebrities is eliminating the wealth legacy or inheritance wealth in order for their children to develop normally and to learn the importance of carving out their own path and being independent. See, for example, Paul, "Bill Gates to Jackie Chan."

path."[12] Qohelet may sort of agree as he fears that whoever inherits his fruit might not be worthy (Eccl 2:18–21). I say "sort of" because, whereas Gates and other wealthy parents want their children to grow up into responsible adults traversing their own path in life, Qohelet demonstrates no concern for whoever receives the fruit of his hard work and success. He is not concerned about spoiling the inheritor but about his own loss.

When we talk about legacy, we usually mean something else, like providing a noble example to emulate or the passing on of some grand vision or passion. Legacy in that sense is more intangible, hoping the next generation will not only continue but even exceed our own efforts and accomplishments. The father or teacher in Proverbs points his child to wisdom, understanding, and knowledge, particularly the fear of the Lord (for example, Prov 1:1–8; 3:12; 4:1; 6:20; 10:1). Paul passes on the gospel to his spiritual children (1 Cor 15:1–8). What legacy do we desire to pass on to the next generation? If our primary focus in our last stage of life is those who follow us, our lives and present efforts assume added significance. Urgency moves us with a sense of purpose; our steps quicken; and each of our days counts.

THOUGHTS ON THE ASIAN PERSPECTIVE ON AGING

The observation that various physical and mental challenges accompany the onset of old age is universal, across cultures. We may recall our younger years with some nostalgia but must grapple with our present reality. Another shared view sees continued good health as the primary contributor to quality of life. Age may be just a number but health or the lack of it can rob one of functionality, joy, and contentment regardless of age.

Among Asians, the family proves quite central. This does not imply that in the West family concerns have no importance; but it is clearer in Asia. Unlike individualistic cultures where the older person envisions travel, embarking on some new adventure, or pursuing some personal dream upon retirement, collectivistic cultures tend to focus more on family relationships, particularly that between grandparents and grandchildren. Before retirement work commitments leave parents little energy for and time with their children. But with retirement, their lives free up significantly and they fill in the gap for their children who are now busy working in caring for their grandchildren. Indeed, several respondents admit to a closer relationship with grandchildren than with their own children. This dynamic

---

12. Paul, "Bill Gates to Jackie Chan," §7.

provides the opportunity to bless the younger generation with the wisdom and experience accumulated over a lifetime. They assume the respected role of teacher, advisor, story-teller, and even playmate. They personify the teacher or mentor in Proverbs.

A few of the elderly have expressed desire for some financial independence in order not to burden their families. They want the freedom to live on their own or have some responsibility within the extended family and not simply be recipients of care and support. This lifestyle preserves their dignity. Quite a few Western blogs espouse self-care routines in order to maintain health and quality of life. Whereas these insights are useful, Asians give more emphasis on meeting the needs of others, particularly younger family members in their formative years. This focus provides a clear purpose of investing in young lives, thereby perpetuating a legacy that will offer continuing dividends in the years ahead, long after one's life is but a memory—a beloved memory.

An important Asian distinction emerges—the attribute of honor and esteem takes precedence over love or being loved, not that the latter is absent. The family deeply respects the elderly and, to some degree, derive their honor or reputation from their elders. In Filipino culture, the younger generation bestows various honorific titles on the elderly, being careful not to call them by first name only. This relational dynamic in Asian cultures helps explain the critical truth behind the biblical admonitions to heed a father's instruction (for example, Prov 1:8; 4:1). The context of the passages cited regard the teachable child "wise" (Prov 1:1–7, 20–23, and 4:2–13). The compatible expression would be "respectful" child in Asia. Obviously, in order for the young to accept the elderly's teaching, they must respect the elder so that wisdom may pass down from one generation to the next. Respect values the experience and wisdom of the old.

In Asia, blessed by honor from the family and society, the elderly may well be living the best years of their long lives. These golden years offer the opportunity to establish a lasting legacy. They model what succeeding generations will emulate and so pass on precious truths and practices that, for Christians, represent Scripture incarnated in yet another generation for the glory of our Lord.

Bibliography

ADB Data Library. "Population and Aging in Asia: The Growing Elderly Population." 2021. https://data.adb.org/story/population-and-aging-asia-growing-elderly-population.

Aetna. "The Secrets of Japan's High Life Expectancy." https://www.aetnainternational.com/en/about-us/explore/living-abroad/culture-lifestyle/the-real-secrets-behind-japans-high-life-expectancy.html.

Agency for Integrated Care. "Active Ageing Centres." 2023. https://www.aic.sg/care-services/active-ageing-centre.

Alter, Robert. *The Wisdom Books: Job, Proverbs, and Ecclesiastes, A Translation with Commentary*. New York: W. W. Norton, 2010.

Bayes, Jonathan F. "The Threefold Division of the Law." *The Christian Institute: Salt & Light Series*. Reprint. (2017) 3–15. https://www.christian.org.uk/wp-content/uploads/the-threefold-division-of-the-law.pdf.

The Business Times. "Raising of Retirement, Re-Employment Ages Will Go Ahead as Planned in 2022." Mar 3, 2021. https://www.businesstimes.com.sg/government-economy/singapore-budget-2021/raising-of-retirement-re-employment-ages-will-go-ahead-as.

Carson, D. A. *Exegetical Fallacies*. 2nd ed. Grand Rapids: Baker Academic, 1996.

Champlin, Edward. *Nero*. Cambridge, MA: Harvard University Press, 2005.

Craigie, Peter C. *The Book of Deuteronomy*. Grand Rapids: Eerdmans, 1976.

Crenshaw, James L. *Old Testament Wisdom: An Introduction*. 3rd ed. Louisville, KY: Westminster John Knox, 2010.

deClaissé-Walford, Nancy L. "The Canonical Shape of the Psalms." In *An Introduction to Wisdom Literature and the Psalms: Festschrift Marvin E. Tate*, edited by H. W. Ballard Jr. and W. D. Tucker Jr., 93–110. Macon, GA: Mercer University Press, 2000.

Di Lella, Alexander A, and Louis F. Hartman. *The Book of Daniel: A New Translation with Notes and Commentary on Chapters 1–9*. AB 23. New York: Doubleday, 1977.

———. *The Book of Daniel: Introduction and Commentary on Chapters 10–12*. AB 23. New York: Doubleday, 1977.

Dong, Xin Qi. "Elder Rights in China: Care for Your Parents or Suffer Public Shaming and Desecrate Your Credit Scores." *Journal of the American Medical Association Internal Medicine* 176.10 (2016) 1429–30. DOI: 10.1001/jamainternmed.2016.5011.

Eastman, David L. "Paul: An Outline of His Life." In *All Things to All Cultures: Paul among Jews, Greeks, and Romans*, 34–56. Grand Rapids: Eerdmans, 2013.

Bibliography

Elsey, Emma-Louise. "The Urgent Important Matrix: What Is It and How to Use It." The Coaching Tools Company, Sep 19, 2023. https://www.thecoachingtoolscompany.com/coaching-tools-101-what-is-the-urgent-important-matrix/.

Eusebius of Caesarea. *Church History*. http://www.documentacatholicaomnia.eu/03d/0265-0339,_Eusebius_Caesariensis,_Church_History,_EN.pdf.

Express Digest. "97-Year-Old Grandmother Becomes a Competitive Weightlifter." https://expressdigest.com/97-year-old-grandmother-becomes-a-competitive-weightlifter/.

Fee, Gordon D., and Douglas Stuart. *How to Read the Bible for All Its Worth*. Imprint ed. Singapore: Campus Crusade Asia Limited, 2007.

Finley, Tom. "Who Wrote the Book of Daniel? Part 2: Who Was Darius the Mede?" *The Good Book Blog, Talbot School of Theology Faculty Blog*, Mar 2, 2022. https://www.biola.edu/blogs/good-book-blog/2022/who-wrote-the-book-of-daniel-part-2-who-was-darius-the-mede1.

Fitzmyer, Joseph A. *Romans: A New Translation with Introduction and Commentary*. AB 33. New York: Doubleday, 1992.

Fox, Michael V. *Qohelet and His Contradictions*. Bible and Literature Series 18. Decatur, GA: Almond, 1989.

———. *A Time to Tear Down and a Time to Build Up: A Rereading of Ecclesiastes*. Eugene, OR: Wipf & Stock, 1999.

Fung, Ronald Y. K. *The Epistle to the Galatians*. NICNT. Grand Rapids: Eerdmans, 1988.

Gallo, Carmine. "Finding the Right Words in a Crisis." *Harvard Business Review*, Apr 17, 2020. https://hbr.org/2020/04/finding-the-right-words-in-a-crisis.

Gilbert, Martin, ed. *Churchill, the Power of Words: His Remarkable Life Recounted through His Writings and Speeches*. Boston: Da Capo, 2012.

Good News Network. "78-year-old Grandmother Goes Viral after Powerlifting 245 Pounds." Apr 5, 2016. https://www.goodnewsnetwork.org/78-year-old-grandmother-goes-viral-powerlifting-245-pounds/.

Gordis, Robert. "Religion, Wisdom and History in the Book of Esther: A New Solution to an Ancient Crux." *JBL* 100.3 (1981) 359–88.

Gorman, Michael J. *Apostle of the Crucified Lord: A Theological Introduction to Paul and His Letters*. Grand Rapids: Eerdmans, 2004.

The Government of the Hong Kong Special Administrative Region of the People's Republic of China SWD Elderly Information Website. "Regulation of Residential Care Homes for the Elderly." https://www.elderlyinfo.swd.gov.hk/en/licensing_regulation.html.

Grogan, Geoffrey F. *Psalms*. The Two Horizons Old Testament Commentary. Grand Rapids: Eerdmans, 2008.

Hamilton, Victor P. *The Book of Genesis, Chapters 18–50*. NICOT. Grand Rapids: Eerdmans, 1995.

Hartley, John E. *The Book of Job*. NICOT. Grand Rapids: Eerdmans, 1988.

Huey, F. B., Jr. "Esther." In *1 & 2 Kings, 1 & 2 Chronicles, Ezra, Nehemiah, Esther, Job*, 773–839. EBC 4. Grand Rapids: Zondervan, 1988.

Iswahyudi, and Bobby Kurnia Putrawan. "Justification by Faith Paul: A Biblical Theological Approach" *International Journal of Social Science Research and Review* 5.5 (2022) 60–66. https://www.academia.edu/80716069/Justification_by_Faith_Paul_A_Biblical_Theological_Approach.

Juneau, Martin. "Why Do the Japanese Have the Highest Life Expectancy in the World?" Prevention Watch, Institut de Cardiologie de Montréal, Mar 9, 2021. https://

Bibliography

observatoireprevention.org/en/2021/03/09/why-do-the-japanese-have-the-highest-life-expectancy-in-the-world/.

Kanfer, Stefan. "Architect of Evil: How Adolf Hitler Mesmerized a Nation—And Terrorized a World." *Time*, Aug 28, 1989, 48–50. .

Kennedy, George A. *New Testament Interpretation through Rhetorical Criticism*. Chapel Hill, NC: University of North Carolina, 1984.

Khalik, Salma. "Singaporeans Have World's Longest Life Expectancy at 84.8 Years." *The Straits Times*, Jun 20, 2019. https://www.straitstimes.com/singapore/health/singapore-tops-in-life-expectancy-at-848-years.

Leveille, Suzanne G., et al. "Aging Successfully until Death in Old Age: Opportunities for Increasing Active Life Expectancy." *American Journal of Epidemiology* 149.7 (1999) 654–64. https://doi.org/10.1093/oxfordjournals.aje.a009866.

Lightfoot, J. B., trans. "The First Epistle of Clement to the Corinthians." In *Early Christian Writings*. https://www.earlychristianwritings.com/text/1clement-lightfoot.html.

Lim, Abram. "The Retirement Age in Singapore and How It Impacts Us." *Smartwealth*, Feb 14, 2021. https://smartwealth.sg/retirement-age-singapore/.

Lim, Puay Ling. "Maintenance of Parents Act." Singapore Infopedia, 2009. https://eresources.nlb.gov.sg/infopedia/articles/SIP_1614_2009-11-30.html.

Lioy, Daniel T. "Teach Us to Number Our Days: An Exegetical and Theological Analysis of Psalm 90." *Conspectus* 5.1 (2008) 91–114.

Liu, Yukun. "China's 'Silver' Economy Grows with Ageing Population." *China Daily, Asia News Network*, Jan 27, 2023. https://asianews.network/chinas-silver-economy-grows-with-ageing-population/#:~:text=According%20to%20the%20Ministry%20of,cent%20of%20the%20total%20population.

Longman, Tremper III. *The Book of Ecclesiastes*. NICOT. Grand Rapids: Eerdmans, 1998.

———. *Making Sense of the Old Testament: Three Crucial Questions*. Grand Rapids: Baker Books, 1998.

Malina, Bruce J. *The New Testament World: Insights from Cultural Anthropology*. 3rd ed. Louisville, KY: John Knox Westminster, 2001.

Matera, Frank J. *Romans*. Paideia: Commentaries on the New Testament. Grand Rapids: Baker Academic, 2010.

Miller, Douglas B. *Symbol and Rhetoric in Ecclesiastes: The Place of Hebel in Qohelet's Work*. Atlanta: SBL, 2002.

Ministry of Manpower. "What Is the Central Provident Fund (CPF)." Apr 25, 2022. https://www.mom.gov.sg/employment-practices/central-provident-fund/what-is-cpf.

Moo, Douglas J. *The Epistle to the Romans*. NICNT. Grand Rapids: Eerdmans, 1996.

Murphy-O'Connor, Jerome. *Paul: A Critical Life*. Oxford: Clarendon, 1996.

Murphy, Roland E. *The Tree of Life: An Exploration of Biblical Wisdom Literature*. 3rd ed. Grand Rapids: Eerdmans, 1990.

Newcombe, Tim. "Howard Hendricks' 4 Bible Study Steps." *Bible Study Magazine* 2.3 (Apr 2010). https://www.crosswalk.com/faith/bible-study/howard-hendricks-4-bible-study-steps.html.

Oshima, T. M. "Nebuchadnezzar's Madness (Daniel 4:30): Reminiscence of a Historical Event or a Legend?" In *"Now It Happened in Those Days": Studies in Biblical, Assyrian, and Other Ancient Near Eastern Historiography Presented to Mordechai Cogan on His 75th Birthday, Volume 2*, edited by A. Baruchi-Unna et al., 645–75. Winona Lake, IN: Eisenbrauns, 2017.

Bibliography

Paul, Trinetra. "Bill Gates to Jackie Chan: Celebrities Who Say Their Children Won't Be Inheriting Their Fortune." *Lifestyle Asia* 2023. https://www.lifestyleasia.com/ind/culture/people/celebrity-kids-who-will-not-receive-inheritance-from-their-famous-parents/#:~:text=Meta%20founder%20and%20CEO%20Mark,t%20be%20inheriting%20their%20fortune.

Payne, Michael. "The Voices of Ecclesiastes." *College Literature* 13.3 (1986) 285–91.

Peticolas, Michelle. "What Is Your Legacy?" Secrets of Life and Death: Embracing the Soul's Dance between Worlds, May 15, 2018. https://www.secretsoflifeanddeath.com/what-is-your-legacy/.

Pinsker, Joe. "When Does Someone Become 'Old'?" *The Atlantic*, Jan 28, 2020. https://www.theatlantic.com/family/archive/2020/01/old-people-older-elderly-middle-age/605590/.

Pritchard, James B., ed. *The Ancient Near East: An Anthology of Texts and Pictures*. Princeton, NJ: Princeton University Press, 1958.

Reis, Rodrigo N. "Justification by Faith: A 'Both-And' Approach." *Channels: Where Disciplines Meet* 1.1 (Nov 2016) 23–41. https://digitalcommons.cedarville.edu/cgi/viewcontent.cgi?article=1000&context=channels.

Renner, Ben. "Study: A Little Weight Lifting Goes a Long Way for Heart Health." StudyFinds, Aug 17, 2019. https://studyfinds.org/study-little-weight-lifting-goes-long-way-heart-health/.

Richards, E. Randolph, and Richard James. *Misreading Scripture with Individualistic Eyes: Patronage, Honor, and Shame in the Biblical World*. Downers Grove, IL: IVP Academic, 2020.

The Royal Australasian College of Physicians. "Integrated Care: Physicians Supporting Better Patient Outcomes, Discussion Paper." Sydney, AU: RACP, 2018.

Sawyer, John F. A. "The Ruined House in Ecclesiastes 12: A Reconstruction of the Original Parable." *JBL* 94.4 (1975) 519–31.

Scazzero, Peter. *Emotionally Healthy Spirituality: Unleash a Revolution in Your Life in Christ*. Singapore: Imprint Edition, 2012.

ScienceDirect editors. "Senility." https://www.sciencedirect.com/topics/neuroscience/senility.

Seow, Choon-Leong. *Daniel*. Louisville, KY: Westminster John Knox, 2003.

———. *Ecclesiastes: A New Translation with Introduction and Commentary*. AB 18C. New York: Doubleday, 1997.

———. *A Grammar for Biblical Hebrew*. Nashville: Abingdon, 1991.

Smick, Elmer B. "Job." In *1 & 2 Kings, 1 & 2 Chronicles, Ezra, Nehemiah, Esther, Job*, 841–1060. EBC 4. Grand Rapids: Zondervan, 1988.

Smith, James P., and Malay Majmundar, eds. *Aging in Asia: Findings from New and Emerging Data Initiatives*. Washington, DC: National Research Council of the National Academies, 2012. N.p. Kindle ed.

Stettler, Hanna. "Did Paul Invent Justification by Faith?" *Tyndale Bulletin* 66.2 (2015) 161–96.

Swanepoel, M. G. "The Important Function of Deuteronomy in the Old Testament." *Old Testament Essays* 5 (1992) 375–88.

Tan, Andrew Kim Seng. "The Rhetoric of Abraham's Faith in Romans 4." PhD diss., University of Cape Town, 2016.

Tsugane, Shoichiro. "Why Has Japan Become the World's Most Long-Lived Country: Insights from a Food and Nutrition Perspective." *European Journal of Clinical Nutrition* 75 (2020) 921–28. https://doi.org/10.1038/s41430-020-0677-5.

Tuo, Jinmei, et al. "Cultural Factors and Senior Tourism: Evidence from the Chinese Context." *Frontiers in Psychology* 13 (2022) 1–9. https://doi.org/10.3389%2Ffpsyg.2022.1030059.

United Nations Department of Economic and Social Affairs. "World Population Ageing 2015: Highlights." New York: United Nations, 2015. https://www.un.org/en/development/desa/population/publications/pdf/ageing/WPA2015_Highlights.pdf.

———. "World Population Ageing 2019: Highlights." New York: United Nations, 2019. https://www.un.org/en/development/desa/population/publications/pdf/ageing/WorldPopulationAgeing2019-Highlights.pdf.

Waltke, Bruce K. *The Book of Proverbs, Chapters 1–15*. NICOT. Grand Rapids: Eerdmans, 2004.

———. *The Book of Proverbs, Chapters 15–31*. NICOT. Grand Rapids: Eerdmans, 2005.

Wang, Xiaojie, et al. "Son Preference and the Reproductive Behavior of Rural-Urban Migrant Women of Childbearing Age in China: Empirical Evidence from a Cross-Sectional Data." *International Journal of Environmental and Public Health* 17.9 (May 6, 2020). DOI: 10.3390/ijerph17093221.

Welocalize. "Evolution of Language across Generations." May 17, 2022. https://www.welocalize.com/evolution-of-language-across-generations/.

Widder, Wendy L. "Letting Nebuchadnezzar Speak: The Purpose of the First-Person Narrative in Daniel 4." *Old Testament Essays* 32.1 (2019) 197–214.

Wilson, Gerald H. "'The Words of the Wise': The Intent and Significance of Qohelet 12:9–14." *JBL* 103.2 (1984) 175–92.

Woo, Jean. "The Myth of Filial Piety as a Pillar for Care of Older Adults among Chinese Populations." *Advances in Geriatric Medicine and Research* 2.2 (Mar 31, 2020) e200012. https://doi.org/10.20900/agmr20200012.

The World Bank. "Population Ages 65 and above (% of Total Population)." 2021. https://data.worldbank.org/indicator/SP.POP.65UP.TO.ZS?end=2021&start=2021&view=map&year=2021.

World Health Organization. "Ageing and Health." Last updated October 1, 2022. https://www.who.int/news-room/fact-sheets/detail/ageing-and-health.

Wright, J. Stafford. "Ecclesiastes." In *Psalms, Proverbs, Ecclesiastes, Song of Songs*, 1135–97. EBC 5. Grand Rapids: Zondervan, 1991.

Wright, N. T. *Pauline Perspectives: Essays on Paul, 1978–2013*. Minneapolis: Fortress, 2013.

Yap, Mui Teng, et al. "Introduction: Aging in Asia—Perennial Concerns on Support and Caring for the Old." *Journal of Cross-Cultural Gerontology* 20.4 (2005) 257–67.

www.ingramcontent.com/pod-product-compliance
Lightning Source LLC
Chambersburg PA
CBHW072149160426
43197CB00012B/2315